W9-CHO-776

STEINBECK

OF MICE AND MEN

AND OTHER NOVELS

NOTES

COLES EDITORIAL BOARD

Bound to stay open

Publisher's Note
Otabind (Ota-bind). This book has been bound using the patented Otabind process. You can open this book at any page, gently run your finger down the spine, and the pages will lie flat.

ABOUT COLES NOTES

COLES NOTES have been an indispensible aid to students on five continents since 1948.

COLES NOTES are available for a wide range of individual literary works. Clear, concise explanations and insights are provided along with interesting interpretations and evaluations.

Proper use of COLES NOTES will allow the student to pay greater attention to lectures and spend less time taking notes. This will result in a broader understanding of the work being studied and will free the student for increased participation in discussions.

COLES NOTES are an invaluable aid for review and exam preparation as well as an invitation to explore different interpretive paths.

COLES NOTES are written by experts in their fields. It should be noted that any literary judgement expressed herein is just that — the judgement of one school of thought. Interpretations that diverge from, or totally disagree with any criticism may be equally valid.

COLES NOTES are designed to supplement the text and are not intended as a substitute for reading the text itself. Use of the NOTES will serve not only to clarify the work being studied, but should enhance the reader's enjoyment of the topic.

ISBN 0-7740-3336-3

© COPYRIGHT 1996 AND PUBLISHED BY
COLES PUBLISHING COMPANY
TORONTO—CANADA
PRINTED IN CANADA

Manufactured by Webcom Limited
Cover finish: Webcom's Exclusive **Duracoat**

CONTENTS

John Steinbeck: Life and Works

John Steinbeck was born in 1902, in the town of Salinas, California. It is generally agreed that the most significant biographical link between Steinbeck and his writing is this fact of his birth and growth to maturity in the Salinas Valley. Here is the source of his knowledge and love of nature, his biological view of life (explained below), and many of his characters, whether the *paisanos* and bums of *Tortilla Flat, Cannery Row* and *Sweet Thursday* or the migrant workers of *In Dubious Battle, Of Mice and Men* and *The Grapes of Wrath*.

Steinbeck lived most of his first forty years in the Salinas Valley, where his mother taught in the public schools of the area and his father was for many years treasurer of Monterey County. (It is said that the author's early novels were written in discarded double-entry ledgers.) Steinbeck's boyhood was probably much like that of Jody in one of his most popular stories, *The Red Pony*. At that time the "long valley" was a series of small farms devoted to cattle raising and the growing of fruit and vegetables, among which were interspersed little towns where the farmers brought their produce to market. Young Steinbeck worked during school vacations for the neighboring farmers and ranchers. Surely these early years of life close to nature form the background from which Steinbeck draws his detailed — and often beautiful — descriptions of natural phenomena. That he attached importance to these youthful experiences in nature can be seen in the following anecdote: at the request of a publisher for early biographical facts, Steinbeck replied that the most important items would probably be of little significance to others; for example, "...the way the sparrows hopped about on the mud street early in the morning when I was little...the most tremendous morning in the world when my pony had a colt."

At the same time, it is clear that Steinbeck read widely, probably through the influence of his schoolteacher mother. Through his fictional characters and other channels (such as correspondence) he had indicated a wide range of reading interests: Walter Scott, Jack London, Robert Louis Stevenson, Dostoyevsky's *Crime and Punishment*, Flaubert's *Madame Bovary*, Hardy's *The Return of the Native*. And it is interesting that he has commented on such reading, "certain books ...

1

were realer than experience ... I read all of these books when I was very young and I remember them not at all as books but as things that happened to me." Such remarks reveal Steinbeck's constant emphasis in his writings upon the concrete and experiential rather than the abstract and theoretical. Steinbeck has also manifested an interest in non-fictional, universally great books, such as the Bible, philosophical literature of ancient India, and Greek historians.

Although he contributed to literary publications both in high school and college (he attended Stanford University for five years as an English major, without taking a degree), the entire period of his young adulthood was intermixed with many experiences in the laboring world. Before beginning courses at Stanford he worked as an assistant chemist in a nearby sugar-beet factory. During the intervals of attendance at Stanford he was employed on ranches and road-building gangs. All of this experience provided first-hand observation of the attitudes, manners and language of the working man, as well as the foundation of his sympathy with the situation of such laborers. Even during a brief stay in New York City (1925-1927), at which point he seems to have definitely decided on a career of writing, since he made unsuccessful attempts to publish stories, he worked both as a newspaper reporter and a laborer, and he financed his return to California by shipping as a deck hand via the Panama Canal. All in all, it is clear that environment, whether the accident of his birth and growth in the Salinas Valley of California, or his own selection of various laboring jobs, figures largely in the source material of Steinbeck's writings.

It should be pointed out that Steinbeck's long residence in the Salinas Valley covered years of both regional and national unrest, changes that he observed and later utilized, especially in his three most sociologically oriented novels: *In Dubious Battle* (1936), *Of Mice and Men* (1937), and *The Grapes of Wrath* (1939). The economic structure of the Salinas Valley itself altered, as small farms were replaced by larger ones and the financial picture enlarged to include corporations, large investments and amassing fortunes. As the gap increased between the little man working for the big man, discontent also increased, resulting in unemployment and threatened strikes. It was all part of the nation-wide economic situation,

2

which culminated in the stock market crash of 1929 and the depression period following. Steinbeck's first published novel, in fact (*Cup of Gold*), appeared two months after the crash. The next few years were especially lean ones for him, as they were for many Americans, although he married, continued writing (with the help of a small subsidy and the house provided by his father), and made the acquaintance of a man who was to exert significant influence on his life for many years to come — Edward Ricketts.

A word or two should be said about Steinbeck's friendship with Ed Ricketts, the marine biologist, which lasted from their acquaintance in the 1930's until Ricketts' death in 1948. Ricketts had a commercial laboratory specializing in marine invertebrates in Pacific Grove, California. He apparently elicited and guided Steinbeck's similar interests in marine biology to specific expression in a work called the *Sea of Cortez* (a record of their joint expedition to the Gulf of California), and toward the general "biological view of life" that pervades much of his writing. (Steinbeck pays special tribute to his friend in the preface to *Sea of Cortez*, in "About Ed Ricketts.") Ricketts is clearly the figure behind some of Steinbeck's most sympathetic portrayals of character (Dr. Phillips in "The Snake," Doc Burton of *In Dubious Battle*, Doc of *Cannery Row* and *Sweet Thursday*), presumably the spokesmen for ideas the two men jointly held. Theirs was an intellectual relationship in which Steinbeck was able to air his views and to arrive at some of his central artistic tenets.

Steinbeck wrote prolifically and variously until his death on December 20, 1968. One of the major changes in his life, however, was his shift of residence from California to New York in 1950. (The decision is often attributed in part to his deep sense of personal loss at the death of his friend Ricketts in 1948.) Significantly, a recent work, *The Winter of Our Discontent* (1961) was set in New England. Also, an account of travels throughout the United States, published in 1962 as *Travels with Charley*, seems to reflect the author's urge in the 1960's toward a revitalization of his creative powers. Steinbeck was awarded the Nobel Prize for Literature in 1962, honored, according to the official wording, for his "realistic and imaginative writings, distinguished as they are by a sympathetic humor and a social perception."

3

List of Major Works

Steinbeck's major works are as follows: *Cup of Gold*, 1929; *The Pastures of Heaven*, 1932; *To a God Unknown*, 1933; *Tortilla Flat*, 1935; *In Dubious Battle*, 1936; *The Red Pony*, 1937; *Of Mice and Men*, 1937; *The Long Valley*, 1938; *The Grapes of Wrath*, 1939; *Sea of Cortez*, 1941; *Bombs Away*, 1942; *The Moon Is Down*, 1942 (this work and *Of Mice and Men* also appear as plays); *Cannery Row*, 1945; *The Pearl*, 1947; *The Wayward Bus*, 1947; *East of Eden*, 1952; *Sweet Thursday*, 1954; *The Short Reign of Pippin IV*, 1957; *The Winter of Our Discontent*, 1961; *Travels with Charley*, 1962. (It should be noted that it is a second version of the Sea of Cortez expedition, published as *The Log from the Sea of Cortez*, 1951, and containing only the "Introduction" and "Narrative" from *Sea of Cortez*, that contains the memorial sketch of Ed Ricketts referred to above.)

Themes in Steinbeck's Works

Biological Theory of Man

Since certain of Steinbeck's attitudes and themes are commonly referred to by critics and recur in most of his writings, including *The Pearl* and *Of Mice and Men*, it is worthwhile to review them briefly before turning to a detailed consideration of the novel at hand. One such attitude has been referred to above as a biological view of man, developed at least in part through Steinbeck's close association with his friend, the marine biologist. Steinbeck relates human beings — his fictional characters — to plants and animals; he seems to see analogies of man in nature, in a manner not so unlike the American Transcendentalists, as represented especially by Emerson and Thoreau, who maintained a mystical reverence for all forms of natural life. His emphasis, of course, is on the natural over the supernatural; but nature in its phenomena and cycles offers even more than simple analogy, Steinbeck seems to suggest. It offers an almost spiritual comfort, and encourages an earth-founded optimism.

Philosophy of Pragmatism, or the Non-teleological

The above term — non-teleological — is often linked with Steinbeck's biological view of man. Steinbeck himself has

4

referred to this "philosophy" — perhaps because of his constantly refreshing urge to communicate to readers by making ideas as concrete as possible — as "is" thinking. As certain critics have explained it, "is" thinking represents "Steinbeck's own attempt to make the technical term *non-teleological* more meaningful to his readers. Broadly, what Steinbeck means is a way of thinking about life that, by concerning itself with what *is*, not with the questions of *why* or *what should be*, avoids the false judgments and exclusions of a squeamish and snobbish morality, and achieves love of life through acceptance." (E.W. Tedlock, Jr. and C.V. Wicker, *Steinbeck and his Critics*.) Such an attitude is very much in the spirit of what the famous American psychologist and philosopher, William James, termed "pragmatism," for pragmatism suggests that a man's thought and his action go hand in hand, and requires that men reason about and judge events as they are experiencing them, instead of applying facilely to their experiences preconceived "why's" and "what should be's." "Is" thinking, or pragmatic thinking, then, recognizes that theoretical or abstract thought does not always fit reality, the way life really happens. To form such a way of thinking into a kind of philosophy, as Steinbeck seems to do, is to express one's belief in a human world of realizable goals, rather than a dream world of impossible ideals.

Steinbeck's Social Consciousness

Although it is perhaps unfortunate for Steinbeck's total literary reputation that the first three of his novels that received serious critical attention were sociologically oriented (since this has caused many critics to read social criticism forcibly into all his works), it is nevertheless true that social consciousness represents a basic element in his writings. This is especially true for *In Dubious Battle* (1936), *Of Mice and Men* (1937), and *The Grapes of Wrath* (1939), all of which were post-Depression novels, and dealt with proletarian matter. The first-mentioned novel is concerned with specific social problems of the period — violence, particularly of strikes and strike-breaking, and the ineffectuality of both "left" and "right" politically speaking, in bringing about more humane conditions and equitable solutions to labor conflicts. The

5

second novel is more involved with men — little men — and their struggles than with generalized social problems. Of this story, about a feeble-minded character, Lennie, and his friend, George, who dream of owning a farm in California, Steinbeck wrote that he was dealing with "the earth longings of a Lennie who was not to represent insanity at all but the inarticulate and powerful yearning of all men." At another time he declared that *Of Mice and Men* was "a study of the dreams and pleasures of everyone in the world," an indication of the continuing emphasis in his writings on the individual man and his strivings rather than stark social criticism. Some of these same issues are also dealt with in *The Pearl*. Even here, though, as in all his works to follow, Steinbeck's focus is upon man; the nature of man and his success and failures, rather than upon the mere detached picture of an indifferent society. (In contrast, for example, to some of Steinbeck's immediate forerunners in American fiction, such as Frank Norris and Theodore Dreiser, who depicted man simply as a wisp in the wind of giant American industrialism and stampeding capitalism.)

Dream and Reality, A Fantasy World

There is an element in Steinbeck's fiction that belongs more to a fantasy or dream world than it does to the real everyday world. Sometimes this element manifests itself in the author's choice of protagonists from among the feebleminded, the castoffs of society and the antisocial. In other instances, it is seen in his descriptions, which often open chapters and conjure up a dreamlike atmosphere (this descriptive quality is especially evident in *Tortilla Flat, Cannery Row* and *Sweet Thursday*). Steinbeck's choice of central characters, in particular, has caused much controversy among critics as to his intentions and the successful realization of them. He has been accused of "glorifying idiocy," (for example, in Lennie, *Of Mice and Men*), or of "deifying the drunk, canonizing the castoff" — the major figures in *Cannery Row*, for instance, by his own stipulation, are society's "nogoods and blots-on-the-town and bums." Similarly, Danny and his friends (in *Tortilla Flat*) live, what by ordinary standards is certainly an unreal existence, surviving more through chance than by planning, and "experiencing" life in a most

6

random way. Or, the characters in *The Wayward Bus* seem selected by the author more for some separate point he wishes to probe about each of them than for the likelihood that they could have, in reality, been thrust together for the rambling bus ride.

We have seen that Lennie, the half-wit (*Of Mice and Men*), was to represent "the inarticulate and powerful yearning of all men . . . the dreams and pleasures of everyone in the world." It is likewise clear from Steinbeck's numerous statements on the book, *Tortilla Flat*, which is episodic (that is, it seems to be a series of episodes strung together, often by dreamlike descriptions), that he intended it to be a kind of modern Arthurian cycle, a story of 20th-century knights of the Round Table, although related in a mock-epic or humorous tone. (The author has spoken, for example, as late as 1957 — *Tortilla Flat* is dated 1935 — of his continuing interest in Sir Thomas Malory's *Le Morte d'Arthur*, and his desire to travel to England to study the manuscript and discuss it with an Arthurian scholar.) Similar objectives outside realistic narrative, along the lines of allegorical symbolic meanings, can be detected in, say, *The Pearl*, which Steinbeck begins with a note on the importance of the parable. These few examples indicate that, however critics may judge his efforts, or however his goals are actually realized, in much of his work Steinbeck is striving beyond realistic narrative or mere social protest, attempting to chronicle, in near-epic form, the struggles of individual men. Those critics who have come especially close to Steinbeck's work, in all its stages (for example, Peter Lisca, E.W. Tedlock, Jr., C.V. Wicker, Warren French) attest to the comprehensiveness and complexity of his style.

7

Introduction to *Of Mice and Men*

In a letter to his publisher in 1938, the year after the publication of *Of Mice and Men*, Steinbeck wrote, "My whole work drive has been aimed at making people understand each other." Though it is in this light that the book should be measured for its ultimate worth, such an evaluation can best be approached if *Of Mice and Men* is read first of all as a story. Most commentators agree that, considered solely as a story, it is a masterly demonstration of the narrator's art. In the first chapter, Steinbeck makes strong suggestions of the action to come. To the experienced reader, he conveys a vague sense of impending doom, and then proves his prowess as a narrator by making what follows both engrossing and suspenseful.

At the same time, he set himself to solve an equally difficult problem in technique. In Joseph Henry Jackson's words, "Steinbeck wanted to write a novel as nearly like a play as he could." He also wanted to re-emphasize some of what he had said in his novel dealing with labor conflict (*In Dubious Battle*, which had appeared the year before, in 1936), but to make his point more sharply, as a statement made within the restricted framework of the theater. In Steinbeck's own words, he wanted to write a "play that can be read or a novel that can be played ... to find a new form that will take some of the techniques of both." It is instructive to compare the novel with the script of the play; except typographically, the differences are far fewer than one would imagine they could be.

Steinbeck worked on the final stage version of *Of Mice and Men*, with some advice from George Kaufman (who directed the play), in the summer of 1937. On November 23, 1937, the play opened on Broadway and was instantly, though not unanimously, acclaimed a masterpiece. That theater season also included *Our Town* (which won a Pulitzer Prize), *The Cradle Will Rock, Golden Boy*, and *Prologue to Glory*, but the Drama Critics' Circle made its award to *Of Mice and Men* on its first ballot.

Stanley Edgar Hyman has made an interesting point regarding the place of this work in the canon of Steinbeck's writing. Hyman begins by dividing Steinbeck's life work into two main periods. The first is concerned with Steinbeck's continuous search for answers to social problems and his

8

rejection of the usefulness of formal religion, pagan rites, amorality, communism and complete individualism. In this first stage of his career, Steinbeck was very concerned with the working class. *Of Mice and Men* represents the turning point in his life work; it is the last book of his first period and the first book of his second. If seen symbolically, according to Hyman, *Of Mice and Men* rejects social solutions. George believes that he can reach utopia and that he can help Lennie reach it. This same kind of belief is held out to the masses by the radical leaders in some of Steinbeck's other novels, and it is a belief, or faith, that is never rewarded. George fails to guide his simple-minded friend, Lennie, into a paradise because Lennie is too unreliable, too simple-minded to be helped. This novel anticipates, at the same time, the novels of Steinbeck's second period by subtly emphasizing the isolation of the individual. George attempts to become part of the landowning class, an effort that comes to nothing, for his ambition, if seen in the context of his temperament and past habits, was ill-conceived to begin with.

Whatever other insights the book may reveal to a reader about Steinbeck's philosophy, it is certain that the simple story of friendship that it tells is a moving statement of the essential decency of humans, and of their essential helplessness. But though it is this, and also an engrossing tale and a playable drama, did Steinbeck succeed as well in the writer's obligatory task of presenting his thesis *through* this story and characters? On this question there has been difference of opinion, and each new reader must, of course, come to his own conclusion.

Of Mice and Men was written at a time when the United States was in the grip of the greatest economic depression it had ever known. There was mass unemployment throughout the land, mass unrest, and the solutions proposed by some were for remedy through mass action. Yet Steinbeck, in this novel, chose to focus his attention on just two of the dispossessed — the unheroic but compassionate George, and George's friend and virtual ward, the mentally defective Lennie. Deliberately sacrificing "bigness" in order to present the plight of the macrocosm (the *mass*) through the microcosm of George and Lennie, Steinbeck said what he had to say about the victims and the nature of injustice in a deceptively simple way. He has expressed concern about the possible

9

failure of his intention: "The microcosm is rather difficult to handle and apparently I did not get it over."

Lennie was particularly difficult to handle. He has been misinterpreted. Steinbeck said that Lennie was not meant to represent insanity, but rather "the inarticulate and powerful yearning of all men." The pertinent question is: does he? It has been said that the character of Lennie is inadequate to this task; yet the almost monstrously pathetic Lennie *is* a sympathetic figure, as are his counterparts, the crippled swamper, Candy; the twisted-back Negro stable buck, Crooks; and even Candy's dog (whose fate, of course, prefigures Lennie's). More important, the character of Lennie is the vehicle through which Steinbeck expresses his thesis.

It is necessary, first of all, that Lennie die — because he is a destructive force, even though he is not responsible for his condition. Like Candy's dog, he must die because, with him, nature has bungled and it is society's responsibility to correct nature's mistakes in order to preserve itself.

Secondly, if Lennie were not the sort of helpless individual he is in the book, the character of George could have been seen only on the same level as all the other ranch hands — as indeed it seems to be when Lennie dies. (It has been suggested, however, that the end of the book predicts a new alliance between George and Slim, the "normal," almost "godlike" member of the class that George was trying to leave.) George accepts the social and humanitarian responsibility of protecting Lennie. Without Lennie, life would be meaningless for George. With him, and with their joint, but never-to-be realized, dream of a farm of their own, life *has* meaning. Though they have nothing else, they have the warm camaraderie of two good friends. As Lennie, in a cry of triumph, says, "We got each other, that's what, that gives a hoot in hell about us."

A few moments after Lennie last utters this triumphant cry, George is compelled to kill his friend. He accepts that social and humanitarian responsibility as well, bitter as it is.

During the conferences preceding the filming of *Of Mice and Men*, a producer suggested to Steinbeck that someone else, not Lennie, should kill the girl, in order to retain audience sympathy for Lennie. Fortunately, this suggestion, which betrays an utter misunderstanding of the book, and a

10

willingness to reduce the story to the lowest level of popular taste, was not carried out.

A line from Robert Burns, "The best laid schemes o' mice and men gang aft a-gley," provided Steinbeck with his title. The whole of the poem from which the line comes is called, *To a Mouse, on Turning up Her nest with the Plough*, November, 1785. The last stanza reads:

> Still thou art blest compar'd wi' me!
> The present only toucheth thee:
> But oh! I backward cast my e'e
> On prospects drear!
> An' forward tho' I canna see,
> I guess an' fear!

Is it too much to suppose that Steinbeck meant this last stanza of the poem, which furnished his title, to stand implicity as George's last statement to his friend and, by extension, to the reader?

Plot Summary

Of Mice and Men is set in California in the 1930s. The story opens on two men who are camping on the banks of the Salinas River. The men are itinerant ranch hands — "bindle-stiffs" — who move around in search of work with their possessions in a "bindle" on their backs. One of them, George, is small, quick and restless; the other, named Lennie, is huge, strong and simple-minded. George acts as something of a guardian to Lennie.

George orders Lennie to give up a dead mouse that he is hiding in his hand. Lennie loves to pet soft things, but because of his tremendous strength, he usually kills them. The two men share a dream. They plan to scrape some money together and buy a small farm: Lennie will be allowed to have soft rabbits to care for; they will own a little house, a garden and "live off the fatta lan'." As George describes the farm, to the delight of the child-like Lennie, we can tell that they talk about it often.

Next day George and Lennie report for work on a nearby ranch. They are greeted by Candy, an old one-armed man who has the job of "swamping" or cleaning out the buildings. They also meet a small, pugnacious man called Curley. Curley, who is the boss's son, takes a dislike to Lennie, for, as Candy explains, Curley "hates big guys. . . . Kind of like he's mad at 'em because he ain't a big guy." Fearing trouble, George has Lennie repeat several times that if anything "bad" should happen, he must go and hide on the riverbank where they had camped the night before.

Curley's wife enters the bunk house. She is pretty, heavily made up and dressed as if for the city. George decides that she is a "piece of jail bait" and warns Lennie to stay away from her.

That evening George talks with Slim, the lead mule driver whose skill at his job and calm, strong personality have made him the recognized leader among the ranch hands. George thanks Slim for giving Lennie a new-born puppy. He talks a little about why he has spent years travelling with his mentally slow friend. Lennie is a "damn nuisance most of the time," but George also values his relationship with the big man. As he explains, "I seen the guys that go around on the ranches alone. . . . After a long time they get mean." He also confides to Slim that they had to leave their last job because Lennie was accused

12

of molesting a girl. Lennie "ain't mean," but he had tried to pet the girl's soft dress and when she objected he panicked and hung on.

That same evening Carlson, another ranch hand, tries to convince the men that the old crippled dog belonging to Candy should be shot. Candy hates the idea of killing his dog: "Had him since he was a pup," he says. The men look to Slim, who favors shooting the animal. Carlson picks up his Luger pistol and takes the dog outside. While Candy turns his face to the wall, the men wait tensely to hear the shot fired.

Candy, alone now, overhears George and Lennie talking about "that little place." He asks if he can team up with them. When Candy reveals that he has some money saved up, the dream of the farm begins to seem possible. We learn that George really does know of a ten-acre farm that is for sale.

Later, Curley takes out his frustrations on Lennie, picking a fight with him. Lennie stands like a helpless child while Curley hits him. George finally shouts, "Get him, Lennie," and the simple giant grabs Curley's fist and crushes his hand. The men take Curley off to the hospital, while Lennie says, "I di'n't mean no harm, George."

The next day, Saturday, most of the ranch hands go into town. Lennie, Candy and Crooks, a black man with a twisted spine, are left behind. So is Curley's wife. Crooks asks if he can join the others on their farm. He will work for free just for a chance to be there. Curley's wife, bored and lonely, saunters by to talk to the three "weak ones." They don't want her around and she retaliates cruelly by lashing out at Crooks.

Sunday afternoon Lennie is sitting in the barn looking sadly at his puppy, which he has just killed by petting it too hard. Curley's wife comes into the barn and sits down with him. She invites him to feel her soft hair. When she tries to get him to stop, he panics, and when she starts to shout, he breaks her neck. Lennie knows he has done "another bad thing" and leaves the barn to go and hide on the riverbank.

Candy finds the girl's body and goes to inform George. They both realize what has happened. The ranch hands form a posse to track down Lennie. George doesn't want him hurt, but Curley is determined to shoot him. Slim points out to George that even if Curley can't find Lennie, the latter will eventually

13

be locked up in an institution. Carlson's Luger is discovered to be missing and Curley thinks Lennie has taken it.

George finds Lennie on the riverbank before the rest of the men get there. He tells him to look across the river and picture the little place they will have one day. While he is telling the familiar story, George pulls the Luger out of his own pocket and shoots Lennie in the back of the neck. When the other men arrive, Curley and Carlson congratulate George for the shooting. They think the gun was fired in self-defence, but Slim knows there was more to it than that, and leads George away.

Characters in the Novel

The Boss: Owner of the ranch. He appears only briefly, and has an arrogant, confident manner that most of the men who work for him lack.

Candy: An old man who lost his hand in an accident on the ranch. He is employed to clean out the buildings, and he fears for the time when he can no longer work. He has a little money put aside. It is Candy's dog that the men decide to shoot.

Carlson: A big, powerful ranch hand. He takes life as it comes and is not particularly sensitive. He owns a Luger pistol.

Crooks: A black man with a twisted spine. He is not allowed in the bunkhouse, but has his own room in the stables. He proudly maintains that it is his right to keep the others out of his room although we learn that he would like company and that this is his way of responding to the fact that he has been rejected.

Curley: An unpleasant, belligerent young man. He is the spoiled son of the boss and likes to pick fights that he can easily win. He has recently married.

Curley's Wife: She is not given a name. She is a young, foolish and pretty girl who tends to brag about men who were going to make her a Hollywood star. Her dreams contrast sharply with her monotonous life on the ranch.

George Milton: An itinerant ranch hand, living in California in the 1930s. He has given his solitary life a sense of purpose by accepting responsibility for his partner, a retarded man. His dream is to own a small farm of his own.

Slim: The leader among the ranch hands. The others look up to him for decisions, and he appears to be tough, wise and kind.

Lennie Small: George's partner, also an itinerant ranch hand. A large man with the mind of a child. He looks at the world innocently with no evil intentions, but since he does not know his own strength he can be dangerous.

Whit: A young ranch hand.

15

Critical Analysis

PART I

Summary

On one side of the warm Salinas River, the Gabilan Mountains slowly rise. On the other, the valley side, trees line the bank. Through the willows and sycamores a path is worn by boys coming down from ranches to swim and by tramps coming off the highway. It is evening of a hot day. A little wind starts to move. Two men emerge from the path and arrive at the narrow pool made by the river. Lennie, the big man, with imprecise features, shambling, flings himself down and drinks from the pool. George is smaller; his eyes are restless. He remembers that Lennie got sick the night before, drinking too much, and warns the big man. George tastes the water carefully, then dabs himself with it. Lennie does exactly the same thing, trying to copy his companion's ritual precisely. They discuss their destination. Lennie has forgotten. He looks in his pocket for his work card, but George reminds him that the smaller man is carrying both. But what is it that Lennie has just taken out of his pocket? Lennie grudgingly gives it to George — a dead mouse. George throws it away, disgusted. Why would anyone want to put a dead mouse in a pocket?

They are going to a ranch, George tells the big man. Once there, Lennie is to shut up. George will do the talking. And Lennie is to behave himself, no "bad things" like he did before. Lennie is sent to get wood so they can start a fire and heat up three cans of beans. He comes back with one small stick of willow and the dead mouse. George had suspected his companion, when he came back with wet feet, of going across the narrow stream to get the mouse. Lennie starts to cry. George, his arm on Lennie's shoulder, explains that getting rid of the mouse is for the big man's own good. They cook the beans.

For the second time Lennie says he wants the beans with ketchup. For the second time George explains there is none, then complains about the burden the big man imposes on him. With no Lennie around, George could save money, never worry, go to a cathouse, go to a poolroom, do anything he

16

wanted. But no. Lennie has to get them into trouble all the time, wanting to pet girls as if they were mice. And then they have to run, hiding in irrigation ditches. George, ashamed of his outburst, looks into the fire. He apologizes. Lennie's Aunt Clara is dead, and George must now take care of the big man.

After a silence, and an increase in the darkness of the evening, Lennie says he really doesn't want any ketchup, wouldn't eat any if he had some right there. As a matter of fact, if George doesn't want him, he'll go right up into the hills and live by himself. No deal, George says; Lennie must stay with his guide. At this point, Lennie asks George for The Story, a tale so often repeated, so similarly repeated that it has become a completely familiar and predictable ritual between the two men. It is the picturing of an ideal future, in which the two companions look after each other, save their money, buy a house, own a cow and some pigs; in which Lennie can play with his rabbits and pet them. Lennie knows The Story so well that he interrupts George in the telling. But the big man will not tell The Story himself. He wants to hear it, to be told the dream — like a child listening to a completely familiar night-time story and delighting in the repetition.

Commentary

In the Viking Press edition of this novel, Part I occupies eleven pages. Probably between 80-90 per cent of this total is written in dialogue. Steinbeck was very much interested in the play form and often referred to it in his correspondence about various works. In addition, the reader will recall the enormous success of *Of Mice and Men* when it was transferred to the stage. It is clear that Steinbeck is trying to fill out his characters by *presenting* them and their speech rather than by *describing* them. He will occasionally interpret some of the action for the reader; he does not rely exclusively upon purely dramatic means. For instance, after the scene in which George angrily explodes and complains bitterly about Lennie's dependence upon him, George looks "ashamedly" at the flames and later stares "morosely" at the fire.

Basically, the narrative technique in this novel is an inheritance from the nineteenth century, the technical tradition of the "omniscient author." What does this mean? It refers to the novelist's technical stance, by means of which —

like an all-seeing god — he assumes full knowledge of the motivations lurking beneath his characters' actions. In addition, he can, at will, turn the reader's attention from one scene to another, distant in space but occurring at the same time, "meanwhile, back at the ranch ..." etc. This technique came into disfavor with many of the most important twentieth-century novelists, impressed by a growing sophistication in the understanding of psychological processes. In other words, a nineteenth-century technique, they felt, would no longer serve to involve contemporary readers in the novel and its characters. Who would *really* believe that a novelist could know what was going on in everybody's mind? Who would *really* believe that a novelist, describing actions, could be in two or three places at the same time?

In an effort to solve the problem, a novelist like Henry James, for instance, would write a novel whose action is perceived *through the eyes and intellect of one particular character.* Such a procedure, though it limits the author's geographical and direct psychological range, allows the reader to understand that most people's behavior is not clearly this or clearly that. When the reader meets the other characters in a novel through the understanding and analysis of one protagonist, a great deal of psychological realism is gained. After all, we must go through life making up our own minds about our fellows, our relatives, our friends and enemies. Sometimes we make mistakes, and often learn about them only after we have committed ourselves to some point of view.

DIALOGUE AND POINT OF VIEW: These considerations, though they may appear to be a digression, constitute important suggestions toward an understanding of Steinbeck's way of writing *Of Mice and Men.* He does not construct this novel so that all the action is directly perceived through only one particular character. Thus, aware to some degree of the weaknesses of the old-fashioned narrative style, Steinbeck utilizes dialogue as a means of seducing the reader into a belief in the reality of the world represented in the novel. Within certain built-in limitations, this process operates quite well in this novel. But such words and phrases as "unhappily," "uncomfortably" and "with dignity" continually show up in the course of the tale. And they tend occasionally to stop the reader in his progress. He is forced to ask: why "uncomfort-

18

ably?'' Through whose eyes is the particular action perceived? Perhaps, thinks the reader, if I were looking at this scene, present in these circumstances, I would not use this adverb; perhaps a dimension of complexity is missing. At one point in this first section, when George asks Lennie what he has in his pocket, Lennie makes a simple denial, "cleverly," as the text reads. Now, according to whom is this statement "cleverly" made? Certainly not according to George, who sees through it immediately. Then it is made in reference to Lennie's own sense of the "cleverness" of his remark. This analysis of an apparently small point emphasizes the running inconsistency of the point of view throughout *Of Mice and Men*, since in many other places in the novel certain adverbial and adjectival modifiers clearly emanate from the omniscient awareness of the novelist.

LENNIE'S SPEECH: But the first part demonstrates Steinbeck's capacity to permit verbal behavior to work toward definition of character. Lennie, with his child's mind, would be expected to talk like a child, and he does. His speech patterns conform to the reader's experience of children's language. A little boy in the question-asking stage of development will include in his queries the name of the "authority." He will ask, "Daddy, why is this wood?" or "Where do the stars go, daddy?" Analogously, a large proportion of Lennie's conversational segments with George include the smaller man's name: "Come on, George. Tell me. Please George..." Another important verbal index of Lennie's developmental age is implicit in his sentence structure and length. George will sometimes speak in complex sentences, involving a relatively subtle sense of subordination, an awareness that one point is more important than another in a particular way, and that several ideas may be put together in one sentence: "You never oughta drink water when it ain't running, Lennie," and "God a'mighty, if I was alone I could live so easy." Lennie, on the other hand, will usually speak in simple or compound sentences, utilizing no more than an "or," an "and," or a "but" to link thoughts. This use of the co-ordinating conjunction is typical of children's speech. When Lennie does use such a subordinating conjunction as "because," implying a greater precision of thought processes, he tends to copy the form after having heard George speak. The

19

reader will isolate such an instance when Lennie interrupts George's hypnotic retelling of The Story. Lennie knows the ritualistic tale so well that he is able to reproduce even George's syntax: "... because I got you to look after me, and you got me to look after you...."

A further aspect of Lennie's speech involves repetition. The big man, at one point, repeats the same sentence, word for word, three times, in an attempt to remember a particular point. In this case, the verbal behavior accents the limited functioning of Lennie's memory. Indeed, his sense of time is rudimentary and cannot clearly differentiate between the present, the past or the future. In this section, the reader already perceives that, for Lennie, reality is a kind of eternal present.

Another representative aspect of Lennie's speech, immediately apparent in this first section, becomes clear particularly in comparison with George's vocabulary. The normal man will use a number of expletives and "substandard" phrases, commonly the products of clashes of wills, frustrations and strains typical of a man's dealing with the world. George will say, "... gives a damn," and "blowin' in our jack ..." and "... you crazy son-of-a-bitch," and "poor bastard." Lennie's speech is singularly free from such phrases. Little boys don't regularly use "bad" language; that happens when they get older. But Lennie will never grow up.

Beyond this list of differences observable in the speech patterns of both men, certain similarities remain, largely involving equal misuse of tenses. George will say, "I been mean ..." and "you ain't gonna...." Lennie's language will include, "... like you done before..." and "... like I seen in the fair...." Steinbeck attempts to indicate pronunciations peculiar to each of the two men, "fambly" for "family," "jus'" for "just," and "som a' the things." But in this intermittent procedure there are inconsistencies: Lennie says "and" as well as "an'."

THEIR PAST: At this point, how much does the reader actually know about either of the two characters? Very few hints about their geographic, socio-economic and religious backgrounds can be found. The most specific indication of a past, and a problem in that past, involves Lennie's Aunt Clara, who is now apparently dead. We learn from bits of conversa-

20

tion between the two men that Aunt Clara had once given Lennie a rubber mouse to play with. Lennie would have nothing to do with it: it "wasn't no good to pet." Lennie's sense of relationships and of time is so poor that he can't even remember her name and calls her "that lady." We know that the two men have been together for a while, but we have no idea how long that period has been. It has obviously been long enough to allow for at least one major breach of the peace by Lennie, whose reflexlike, unthinking tendency to pet anything soft — in that case an unwilling girl — touched off an immediate and frightened escape from their last job. They had had to run, and worse, to hide while they tried to shake off their pursuers.

THEIR CLOTHES: Do their clothes tell us anything about them? This line of inquiry is not too helpful. They are both dressed in denim trousers and coats with brass buttons. They both wear black, shapeless hats. They both carry blanket rolls over their shoulders. Besides identifying the men as travellers, and poor ones who are not city people, their apparel tells us little. They are introduced to the reader as "losers," and it is partly their clothes, as well as their own sense of themselves, which probably induced the bus driver to misinform them about the precise location of the ranch. Lennie is too lacking in insight to make such observations, but George, for all his deprivation, has enough pride to realize the bus driver's discourtesy and to comment on it.

PART II

Summary

Fortified by Lennie's promise that in case of any trouble he would hide out in the brush by the river, George heads for the ranch bunkhouse. It is a long, rectangular building containing eight bunks. An apple box is nailed over each bunk to provide shelving for personal belongings. A big, cast-iron stove and a big table are in the middle of the room. An old man leads the pair in, telling them that the boss is angry because they had not come the previous evening. It is now 10 a.m. He shows them their bunks. George looks into his apple-box shelf and notices a can of louse- and roach-killer. "What the hell's this?" he says. The old man goes through an elaborate series of assurances, all testifying to the extraordinary, even obsessively scrupulous cleanliness of the last inhabitant of the bunk. "Why, he'd put that stuff down even if he saw nothing, no bugs or anything. That's the kind of a guy he was." George, still suspicious, looks under the mattress. (Lennie immediately does the same thing with *his* bed.) Satisfied, George starts to put his things away. In conversation, the old man mentions the stable hand, a Negro, who serves as the boss' scapegoat when the owner gets angry at something else — like the lateness of Lennie and George.

The door opens. It is the boss. He takes their names, asks them questions, but George answers for both. The boss resents this procedure, and suspiciously wonders out loud about the quality of George's interest in Lennie. He finally accepts them. They are to work on Slim's team in the fields, picking barley with a thresher. The boss leaves and the old man returns, followed by an old sheep dog, moth-eaten and tired. Curley enters, asking for his father, the boss. He goes over to Lennie and asks him to identify himself. The big man doesn't speak and Curley and George almost come to blows until George allows Lennie to say a few words. After Curley's departure, the old man briefly discusses Curley's general lack of a sense of justice. Curley has been married for two weeks, the old man adds, and his wife is already giving others "the eye." A nasty situation might be brewing. George impresses upon Lennie the absolute necessity of staying away from Curley. Suddenly, Curley's wife is standing in the doorway.

22

Lennie is fascinated and watches her carefully She throws her body forward by leaning against the door frame. She leaves quickly upon hearing from Slim, who is walking by, that her husband is home. " . . . what a tramp," George says. But Lennie has fallen for her. George fiercely warns Lennie to stay away from her.

At this point, Slim enters, talks gently to the two men and smiles appreciatively when George compliments Lennie on his capacity for work. Another man comes in. His name is Carlson, apparently another hand. He tells Slim that the dog belonging to the old man — Candy — should be shot. The dog has no teeth, is almost blind and smells. Slim has a dog and five pups. He could give Candy one of the pups as a substitute. Lennie excitedly asks George to have Slim give him one of the pups. They all start out for chow when Curley stalks in looking for his wife. He scowls and leaves.

Commentary

This entire part takes place in the bunkhouse. If it were a play script, it couldn't have been written in a manner more useful for the stage. The formal structure is extraordinarily simple and direct. After the two men have entered the bunkhouse, preceded by Candy, every single new character enters by the same door, one at a time. Seen abstractly, this formal procedure smacks of artifice; but the fact is that the bunkhouse *is* the center of life in the ranch, and that the entries and departures do not lack verisimilitude. In addition, there is inherent in the part an almost formal or ritualistic process, a sequence of more or less deliberate entrances and exits into and out of the small world of the bunkhouse. Ritual is more readily thought of in the case of poetry and poetic drama, than in prose. But the reader will gain a greater understanding of this section if he recalls that Steinbeck, although nominally placed in the "realistic" novel tradition by general consent, also manifests in a number of works a strongly poetic sympathy — not only with the processes of nature, but with the relationships between men as well.

It is true that the Introduction has discussed Steinbeck's preference for the "biological point of view," but it has also pointed out the particular qualities that he admires in the *paisanos* he often wrote about. And those qualities involve

23

modes of ritual — courtesies, devoted enjoyment of natural processes, admiring concern for sexuality, a pattern of warmhearted appreciation of goodness outside a concern for property. These are merely instances. Mainly, these considerations attempt to bring the reader's attention to an aspect of Steinbeck's thought as it works itself out in a particular context. No reader will mistake the degree to which George and Lennie are different, physically, verbally and mentally. But, although Steinbeck succeeded here in creating believable characters, these characters also operate as symbols. In such a novel, for instance, as *The Moon is Down*, the novelist created types instead of people, and thus lost not only the reader's belief but also the reader's involvement in any other level. In this novel, both George and Lennie come across, generally, as believable figures, *and* they belong in a scene that is characterized as well by the presence of a kind of symbolic shorthand.

OF MICE AND MEN AS ALLEGORY: Typically, instead of demonstrating to the reader the temperament and moral stance of a particular character by a slow and continuous sequence of ten or twenty social involvements, Steinbeck here chooses one anecdote, one telling trait, one item of clothing and allows each to take on symbolic power in the definition of the *essential* quality of a person. This is the reason why *Of Mice and Men* has an allegorical quality. That is to say, the novel tends to single out primary character traits. Such a procedure makes the book vulnerable to accusations of superficiality and dubious simplicity. A person, after all, is not just the representative of one or two attitudes, but of many, and what matters is the total. But if the reader accepts the somewhat allegorical mode of *Of Mice and Men*, he will experience a greater sympathy for it. We may find in certain specific aspects of this part some illustrations of our general statements.

THE BOSS AND CURLEY: We find in Part II only two references to the boss, both short, both conveyed by Candy, the old man. He first tells George that when the boss gets angry, he takes it out on the Negro stable hand. The reader gets the impression that the Negro is a kind of whipping boy. Right after that statement, Candy tells a story about the boss, who showed his generosity the previous Christmas by bringing in a gallon of whiskey to the bunkhouse and then told

24

everyone to drink up. And in the jollity that followed, the stable hand was allowed to come into the bunkhouse from his own room in the harness room. There was a fight for everybody's amusement, between the stable hand and another worker. Since the Negro had a hunchback, the worker was forbidden to use his feet in the fight — in the interest, apparently, of a sporting match. The fact that the stable hand won seems quite clearly secondary to the reader's impression of the hidden and manipulative malice operating from the top down.

It is directly after the telling of this story that the boss walks in. And his behavior with George and Lennie in their brief conversation together derives its overtones largely from what the reader has just found out. Another character in this part is defined through the mention of one carefully observed trait, which comes up three times in the course of two and one half pages. Curley, the boss' son, is described only generally — thin, young, brown eyes, tightly curled hair — but the author notes that he wears a work glove on his left hand. The reader senses him immediately as an unpleasant character.

After his very brief visit to the bunkhouse, Curley leaves. Candy, the old man, talks about him, tells George that the boss' son has done quite a bit in the ring and is very handy with his fists. The old man continues by stating that if Curley jumps someone, a bigger man, and licks him, everybody praises him as a "game guy." On the other hand, if Curley loses, everybody says that the bigger man should have picked on someone his own size. By this time, the reader, remembering the image of the glove on the left hand, has begun to conceive of that glove as a symbol. The final allusion to Curley's glove, also made by the old man, discloses the information that it is filled with vaseline — Curley is keeping his hand soft for his wife, according to the old man. Thus, the poetic value of the glove is increased. To the reader's sense of Curley as an unjust, immoral creature of power, is added the almost obscene suggestiveness of some of the qualities of the vaseline: smoothness, secrecy, cloying and hidden effeminacy.

CANDY, THE OLD MAN: The old man is an interestingly conceived character. On occasion, Steinbeck will not tell the reader the names of some of his protagonists. Sometimes this lack appears appropriate in the context of a particular work. At other times, it leaves a vacuum. With the lack of specific names comes a lack of a sense of reality. The reader meets "Curley's wife," in this part, for instance. He does not learn her name, nor does he know whether he will find it out later or not. He does discover the old man's name, but only on the next-to-last page of this section. Until that point, he's just "the old man."

Whether by design or by intuition, Steinbeck would seem to have taken some hints from the function of the classical Greek chorus in the use of Candy. In ancient Greek drama, the chorus, identified no more specifically, sometimes represents the direct response of the people in general, sometimes attains to a further moral level in which it comments upon the action, attaches blame and praise. The old man, analogously, is relatively anonymous at first. He seems to represent a generalized level of moral blindness on the part of the bunkhouse hands when he acclaims the boss' generosity in bringing whiskey to his men once a year. And he does not *directly* accuse the boss of blame in the subsequent fight between the worker and the Negro. Later in this part, however, Candy does point the finger at Curley, deploring the moral laxity of the boss' son. It is interesting that it should be this very man, Candy, who is directly involved in the first symbol of impending death in the novel. Near the end of Part II, in the same paragraph that discloses Candy's name, the worker, Carlson, also makes his suggestion that the old man's dog should be shot. Thus, as we see, another poetic aspect of this section arises from our examination.

CLOTHES AND THE MAN: We have seen that very little, if anything, could be derived from the clothes Lennie and George wore when we first met them at the pool. In this part, the way people are dressed does play into the reader's reaction to the characters. The order in which they appear follows:

a. the old man
b. the boss
c. Curley, the boss' son
d. Curley's wife
e. Slim
f. Carlson

26

Accidental or not, an interesting linear structure reveals itself here. The author describes the clothing of the first character — the old man — only minimally. The same lack of description holds for the last — Carlson. Aside from certain direct statements concerning moral worth (particularly in reference to Slim), articles of personal dress, as well as hair, ornamentation and so forth, tend to suggest attitudes on an ethical level. We know that the old man wears blue jeans and carries a big push broom. That's all. We know that Carlson is a "powerful, big-stomached" man. That's all for him. But the boss, we are told, is a little man, a stocky man. He wears blue jean trousers, a flannel shirt, a black vest (unbuttoned) and a black coat. His thumbs are in his belt, he wears a Stetson hat and, most importantly, he wears high-heeled boots in order to prove, as the author tells us, that he is not a laborer.

The reader is prepared to dislike the boss. The old man has just described the incident of the gallon of whiskey. And, thus, the unsubtle comment about the high-heeled boots begins to draw the reader's sympathy away from the managerial, propertied symbol, and toward the workers. As for Curley, who enters next, besides the glove, he also wears exactly the same kind of boots as his father. In addition, he has a head of "tightly curled hair," which, without too much forcing of similarity, can be interestingly compared to his wife's hair, done up "in little rolled clusters." Both are hair *styles*, products of artifice and, thus, in the common moral world of Steinbeck's fiction, undesirable. In addition, Curley's wife wears heavy lipstick, red fingernails and red shoes decorated at the insteps with little bouquets of red ostrich feathers. Her voice is nasal and "brittle."

As for Slim, the next to enter, *his* hair is long, black and damp. At the very moment that he enters, he is engaged in combing it straight back. Slim does not wear high-heeled boots. We are told only that he has on blue jeans and a denim jacket and a Stetson. But, here, the narrator departs from his pattern to discuss Slim's moral virtues abstractly. He walks with a majesty found only in "royalty and master craftsmen," is able to kill a fly on a horse's rump with his whip without touching the animal, has a manner so grave and profound that all talk stops when he speaks. His speech is slow and welcomes understanding. His face, a "hatchet face," lean, is ageless. His

27

hands are large and lean. He is "the prince of the ranch." And, with that one word, "prince," we perceive the particular quality of this novel again. Of course, we think, an allegory, a fairy tale, perhaps even a piece of an old epic story in which good and bad can be readily identified. The wonder is that such realizations do not make us stop reading; but the narrative continuity is skilfully worked. And even if we know, or think we know, what the ending will bring, the story is not completely the thing. As in rituals, we remain fascinated by the roll of events, the clash of good and evil, innocence and experience, and we give ourselves to the old story once more.

THE VERBS: Even the verbs used in the description of manner of entry into the bunkhouse play their part in setting up the characters in a kind of storied light. Both the old man and Carlson "came" into the bunkhouse. As for the boss, Curley, Curley's wife and Slim, other means are required to enhance their dramatic stature. Steinbeck's procedure is very simple, and very effective. The boss does not simply "come in," he "stood in the open doorway." Curley's wife cuts off the rectangle of light in the doorway, and is "standing there." Slim "stood in the doorway." To *stand* in an open doorway, one's back to the source of brilliant light, is to be framed like a portrait, to be arrested in time, and heightened. What about Curley? He appears twice in this scene. At first, he merely "came" into the bunkhouse; but in his last appearance, near the end of Part II, he "bounced in." As we shall see later, Curley represents the active principle in the tragic development of the novel.

MORAL HIERARCHY: The reader might speculate here about a possible scale of moral perception in which these characters are involved. Directly and indirectly Slim constitutes the high point of such a hierarchy. He looks at the two men "kindly," he talks to them "gently," his tone is "friendly" and invites confidence "without demanding it." And, implicit in this last citation lies the kernel of Slim's moral ascendancy. He does not demand, or manipulate; he is not self-seeking, has no vested interest. He derives satisfaction from his physical work, which he does supremely well, and does not ask for reassurance from others. Curley's wife wants recognition, wants flirtation and wants commitments of interest. The boss wants reassurance too. His suspicious nature

28

cannot rest satisfied with its own perceptions. He is on the lookout for trouble. He wants to be told about the relationship between Lennie and George. He does not want to be fooled. He wants to keep on top of everything. He wants to impress the pair with his power. Curley, more extreme than his father, wants even more. He wants to manipulate physically. He wants to set up situations for testing his strength, about which he is unsure. He wants not only recognition, but deference. It is interesting to note that, if Slim constitutes the high level of ethical perception in the scene, the other significant moral generalization made is uttered by Lennie, who says, "Le's go, George. . . . It's mean here." Although the big man lacks complexity, he is apparently able in his gross and untutored way to act as a moral antenna. Whether or not in strict terms of mental development this perception is believable, is a question. However, Lennie's comment certainly underlines Steinbeck's frequent note of the sham in social forms and the corresponding goodness in simplicity.

PART III

Summary

It is evening. In the bunkhouse it is dusk, even though evening brightness shines through the windows. Slim and George enter together. George thanks the other man for his gift of the puppy to Lennie. They sit down on boxes. After Slim admiringly mentions Lennie's immense capacity for work, he comments about the closeness between the pair. Such loyalty is unusual, he feels. George explains that he is now filling a kind of guardian role, after the death of Lennie's aunt. George experiences a feeling of trust for Slim. He tells about the incident in their previous place of employment. Slim simply asks if the girl got hurt, and adds that Lennie is not mean.

Lennie walks in, hunched over. George immediately tells him not to bring his pup into the bunkhouse. After some complaining Lennie takes the pup back. Candy and Carlson enter. The latter again suggests that Candy's dog is better off dead. Although the dog is old, blind and smelly, Candy desperately counters Carlson's suggestion. For the first time Slim speaks up. He agrees with Carlson, and will give Candy one of the pups as a substitute for the old dog. Carlson, despite Candy's plea to wait for the next day, takes a luger pistol out of his clothes bag. Candy yields. Carlson takes the dog out. Slim reminds him to take a shovel and says he must put some tar on a mule's hoof. A shot sounds, and Carlson rolls over on his bunk.

Crooks, the Negro stable hand, enters. He's got the tar from Slim, and reports that Lennie is messing around with the pups. Slim and Crooks leave. Whit, a young laborer who had come in just before, talks to George about Curley's wife and the trouble she might stir up. He also invites George to a whorehouse in the vicinity, cheap drinks and good, clean girls. George might go for a drink sometimes, but no more; he needs the money for the house he wants to get with Lennie.

Lennie and Carlson come in. The latter cleans his gun. Curley bursts in, looking for his wife, and asking for Slim's whereabouts. He then rushes out to the barn to see Slim. George, Candy and Lennie are left alone when Whit and Carlson go out to see what's going to happen. George and

30

Lennie talk about their dream house and farm. Candy suddenly asks where such a house might be located. George answers ambiguously and then tells the old man the house would cost $600. Candy, who had lost one hand working on the ranch, got compensation for his accident. He says he will donate a total of $350 if he can be included in the project. George and Lennie, amazed and happy, accept and swear the old man to secrecy.

Slim and Curley, Whit and Carlson walk in. Slim, Carlson, and even Candy attack Curley for his lack of control of his wife. Lennie, still smiling absently at the memory of the ranch, infuriates Curley, who punches him in the face. The big man retreats, terrified. George stops Slim from interfering and yells to Lennie: " . . . get him." Lennie seizes Curley's swinging fist and crushes it. Slim notes that almost every bone in Curley's hand is broken. He warns the boss' son not to say how it happened, at the risk of becoming the laughingstock of the ranch. Carlson, who had left to get a doctor, comes back in a buggy. Slim leads the wounded man outside. "It ain't your fault," George tells Lennie, and tells him to wash his bloody face.

Commentary

The setting in this part is the same as that in the previous one. However, here the action begins to pick up. Like a good playwright, Steinbeck has introduced most of the important characters to the reader by the time this part begins, and the narrative can now go forward a little more rapidly.

THE IMPORTANCE OF SLIM: In both of the major episodes in the part, the central figure is Slim. He is central in the contexts of morality, authority and self-respect, not in terms of pure physical activity. Carlson's continual complaints about the old man's smelly dog might have had no concrete effect had it not been for Slim's intervention. In the second event, the dispute with Curley, probably neither Carlson nor Candy would have dared to attack Curley verbally without Slim's tacit agreement. And it is these verbal assaults that move Curley to take cowardly revenge on Lennie, who had had absolutely nothing to do with the situation.

So we must turn our attention more intensively to Slim, the "prince," who appears to be involved in the entire part in a

31

consistent and essential manner. That he is merely the central figure, however, is debatable. Slim's roles could be effectively compared with those of a psychoanalyst and a judge. The patience and professional passivity of the first can be contrasted with the legal involvements required of the second.

SLIM'S CHARACTER: In the beginning of Part III, George finds it possible to tell Slim his most incriminating secret, the story of what happened in the town of Weed, when Lennie got into trouble. Slim makes an apparently idle comment expressing interest in the closeness between the two men, but he does not *ask* any questions. This is the second occasion during which the matter has come up. On the first, early in Part II, the boss immediately communicates his disbelief in George's capacity for disinterested and sincere concern for Lennie. For the boss, a belief in such qualities would lead to a weakening of those traits that establish him as an owner, hirer and manipulator. In Slim's case, such a belief is part of the personality. It also contributes to his use as a primitive, ethical symbol. A "real smart guy," he says at one point, "ain't hardly ever a nice fella."

But his main attitude in the early part of this scene is represented by his tone. His comment about the two men is a "calm invitation to confidence." When George, eager to talk but wary, remains momentarily silent, Slim "neither encouraged nor discouraged him. He just sat back quiet and receptive." Slim's comment after a particular disclosure by George is "Ummm." At one point, George starts to tell Slim what happened in Weed. Alarmed at the confidence he is about to communicate, he stops. Slim asks a simple question here, but "calmly." Slim's eyes are "level and unwinking," he nods "very slowly." Again, his "calm eyes" follow Lennie out the door when the big man goes to return the pup.

Almost superhuman in his wisdom and detachment, this is the Slim whom the reader can envision in the role of the psychoanalyst. All comparisons fall down somewhere, but this one is useful enough to be considered. The classical analyst will, like Slim, allow the patient time in which to come to a sense of ease. He will also adopt a non-directive role toward the patient. That is, the analyst will not impose upon the patient a moral system, approvals and disapprovals as a requirement for the continuation of the relationship.

32

At this point, however, a major difficulty intrudes itself upon the reader's experience of the section. It is true that Slim's benevolent detachment leads to some heart-warming results. But Slim's previously cited comment about the relationship between a "real smart guy" and "a nice fella" emphasizes the presence of a "non-objective" point of view. This inconsistency, and its tendency toward over-simplification, has been noticed by a number of critics. The situation may become a little clearer in focus if the reader recalls the importance of Edward Ricketts in the life of John Steinbeck. We have seen that a number of important characters in various Steinbeck novels — *Cannery Row*, for instance — are modelled after the marine biologist. Important among the qualities that the novelist most admires is the scientist's objectivity. And this objectivity co-exists with the awareness and acceptance of biological processes, in which the old must die, the young get old, and one generation must give way to the next. This commitment is impersonal and does not supply a valid basis for such opinions as Slim's, previously cited. When Slim says, "That dog ain't no good to himself. I wisht somebody'd shoot me if I get old and a cripple," he is speaking out of the second half of the paradox, which is his nature. His acceptance of biological necessity clashes with his sentimental attitudes of mind.

INCONSISTENCY IS HUMAN: The reader may counter some of these objections to Slim's inconsistencies by asserting that: (1) a human being is not a philosophy, and does not have to be held accountable for perfectly logical and self-consistent attitudes. After all, Emerson did say that "a foolish consistency is the hobgoblin of little minds."; (2) Slim's attitudes function as synthesizing and binding roles within the structure of this part. And, since the structure of a work of literature implies its own meaning, Slim's relationship to this structure is informative.

SLIM'S FUNCTIONAL ROLE: As an illustration of the relevance of this second point, we may look more closely at the scene dealing with the problem of Candy's old dog. What are the arguments that are marshalled by the old man in support of his desire to keep the animal? He's been around the dog so long that he does not notice the stink; he's had the dog so long and likes him so much that he can't stand not being

33

with him; his memory of the old dog's prowess as a sheep dog compensates for the dog's present paralysis; he doesn't mind taking care of the dog; the shot might hurt the dog. Carlson, the animal's archenemy, counters all these objections: the dog's no good to Candy; it stinks "to beat hell"; the animal's all stiff with rheumatism; the dog's no good to himself; Candy is being cruel to the dog by keeping it alive; the shot would not hurt the dog for even one second.

Structurally, Slim's arbitration of the situation is worthy of Solomon: the dog is no good to himself; but Candy is to get another one. Although Slim is not the first to suggest that the old man take one of the pups, and although he is not the first to suggest that the dog is no good to himself, he does make one very important observation, unique to him. Slim comments that he wishes somebody'd shoot him if he ever gets old and crippled. Thus, by including himself in the human situation, Slim effectively counteracts both the harshness of his own biological dictum *and* the harshness of Carlson's self-righteous demands. Ironically, Slim himself is the living refutation in this instance of his previous statement that intelligence and generosity do not go together.

GEORGE AND THE MORAL SENSE: At one point in Part III, George finds it possible to tell Slim a story of the greatest importance in the development of the relationship between Lennie and his companion. The tale is significant not only on the level of human connections, but stands out as a kind of fable of moral propriety, concerned with the uses of power. The growth of an ethical sense implies the renunciation of the use of power in many instances, when such use can be perceived as hurtful to other human beings. George tells Slim that one time a group of "guys" were standing along the bank of the Sacramento River. George, feeling "pretty smart," turned to Lennie and ordered him to jump in. Although he could not swim, Lennie immediately obeyed — and nearly drowned before the group recovered him from the water. And then, George adds, Lennie was nice to him for pulling him out. "I ain't done nothing like that no more."

This circumstance holds little ambiguity. Its moral point is clear. Later on, in Part III, however, an incident occurs that questions the constant capacity of any man — no matter how full of good will — to adequately make decisions about the

34

proper and improper uses of power, especially in an urgent situation. After Curley first struck Lennie in the nose, the big man retreated to the wall. Slim, disgusted and infuriated by the illegitimate assault, jumped up cursing Curley, and saying, "I'll get 'um myself." George had an important decision to make on a split-moment basis. He had already told Lennie to "get" Curley, and the big man had been too frightened to respond appropriately. At this point, would it not have been a sound idea to allow Slim to take care of Curley? George knew that Lennie, once enraged, was uncontrollable. He knew that Slim could dispose of the boss' son. He did not simply ask Slim not to mix in, he "put out his hand and grabbed Slim. 'Wait a minute,' he shouted." An objective observer might note that George's personal desire for revenge against Curley, whom he already disliked, overruled a more sensible course of action. In addition, since George did not know when Lennie would finally respond to his companion's permission to strike back, the big man might very well suffer greater punishment than if Slim had immediately interceded. If the analysis is pursued further, a reader might even wonder about the possibility that George's choice might have been — ever so slightly — determined also by his covert hostility to Lennie. After all, the "brainy one" of the two had on several occasions complained grievously about the burden that Lennie constituted. Whatever the truth, and however solid George's active good will might appear, the incident suggests the imperfection of the moral sense in a complex and urgent situation. And, as we shall see, Curley's indelible hatred for Lennie, as a result of this incident, plays a very significant part in the tragic outcome of the narrative.

SLIM AS EPIC HERO: We have spoken of George's confession to Slim as a fable of moral propriety. This fabular, or legendary, sense is also implicit, of course, in the person of Slim. The repeated use of such adjectives as "calm," such adverbs as "gently," "kindly," remind us of much earlier patterned usages, like those of Homer. The old epic poems typically contained a horde of repeated epithets, which helped to isolate and define individual characters. "The wine-dark sea," Homer would write, extending epithets even to inanimate aspects of nature. The heroes and heroines in old epic poems were a cut above ordinary human beings. They

35

were stronger, more courageous, handsomer and more perceptive. Slim can be identified as a member of such a company. But even the hero is subject to the law of the gods, and the will of the gods. In *Of Mice and Men*, Slim, helpful, concerned and involved as he may be, is nevertheless another pawn in the impersonal processes of fate. He is the one who immediately thinks of getting a doctor for Curley; he is the one who examines Curley's hand; he is the one who convinces Curley not to talk about the incident; he is the one who helps Curley out of the door to the waiting buggy. But even he "regarded Lennie with horror," as if the big man, in some mysterious and paradoxical way, himself represented the unknown machinations of power beyond analysis.

TENSION: This part is characterized by a great deal of tension. Between the discussions about the dog (and Carlson's act), and the entrance of Curley, intervenes a scene that adds a great measure of poignancy to the sensed overtones of future disaster in the end of the entire part. On no less than four separate occasions, within the space of five pages, George says, "Me and Lennie's gonna roll up a stake;" "Me and Lennie's rollin' up a stake;" "Lennie and me got to make a stake;" "We gotta get a big stake together." The reader, unsure as to whether the $600 house and land really exist, involved sympathetically with the hope newly born in the pair and Candy, reacts all the more actively in the context of the violence at the end of Part III.

PART IV

Summary

The Negro stable hand, Crooks, lives in the harness room, a shed leaning off the wall of the barn. He sleeps on a box filled with straw. Broken harness and tools of the trade hang on wall pegs. A number of personal belongings are scattered about the floor. Crooks lives alone and has no need to concern himself with the placement of his belongings. In addition to several pairs of shoes, boots, a clock and a shotgun, he owns some books: a torn dictionary and an old copy of the California civil code of 1905. He owns gold-rimmed glasses, which hang on a nail. On this Saturday night, Crooks is sitting on his bunk, rubbing his spine with liniment. The harness room is dimly lit with one small bulb.

Lennie walks in quietly. He smiles and Crooks tells him curtly that he has no right to be in the harness room. Crooks understands Lennie's sense of aloneness — everybody's gone into town, including George. The Negro finally allows Lennie to sit for awhile. They talk. Lennie tells the hand his dream. Crooks asks Lennie what he would do if George did not come back. Lennie becomes threatening, and the Negro changes his line of questioning and complains about loneliness. He reminisces about his childhood with his two brothers, his alfalfa patch and his berry patch. George and he will have rabbits and a berry patch, Lennie tells Crooks. Nobody ever gets that little piece of land, according to the stable hand; hundreds of men come off the roads, onto the ranches, all dreaming the same dream about the little piece of land and none of them ever gets it. Candy suddenly comes by, and despite his embarrassment, comes in. It's the first such visit to Crook's room. Only Slim and the boss have ever come into it before. Upon Crook's repeated insinuation that the land will never materialize, Candy tells him that the money is already available. Almost convinced, and nearly believing, Crooks asks to be let in on the deal. At this point, Curley's wife comes in, looking for her husband and complaining about the boredom from which she suffers. She asks about Curley's hand. It got caught in a machine, Candy explains. She does not believe this story. She's not a child, to be told lies; why, she could have been "in pitchers." And now she's reduced, on

37

this Saturday night, to a conversation with "a nigger, an' a dum-dum and a lousy ol' sheep —"

Candy, surprisingly, stands up and angrily attacks her for her lack of understanding. She doesn't realize they are not "stiffs." They will be landowners. She doesn't believe it. Candy controls himself and simply advises her to leave. He doesn't care whether she believes them or not. She looks at Lennie's face, asks him where the bruises come from. He stammers that Curley got his hand caught in the machine. She says that she likes machines. "O.K. Machine. I'll talk to you later." There is some banter about rabbits. She seductively tells Lennie she might get a few herself, whereupon Crooks stands and faces her. He's had enough. She must leave. Furious, she turns upon him and threatens him with dire retribution if he ever talks to the boss about her. Crooks retreats within himself and blots out his personality. Candy says they would tell that she framed Crooks if she lied about the stable hand. Nobody would listen, she says. She leaves, with a final thanks to Lennie for "busting up" Curley. George, returned, calls for Lennie, and comes to Crooks' door. He disapproves of Lennie's visit. Crooks says it's all right: Lennie's a nice fellow. Candy says he's figured out how to make money from the rabbits. George's displeasure is clear when he hears that Candy told someone about the plan. Candy says he told nobody but Crooks, who calls to the old man and takes back his suggestion that he come in on the land. Crooks wouldn't want to go to any place like that. The three men leave and Crooks rubs his back again.

Commentary

Here, in this part, we find gathered together the disinherited of the world, the isolated, men born — as is sometimes said — under the wrong star. The scene derives a certain portion of its power from an internal paradox. And it is the figure of Lennie that operates as the center of this paradox. As Slim, in the previous part, constituted the synthesizing force, so in this part, Lennie operates analogously. The reader senses an almost mystical belief in the social effectiveness — under appropriate conditions — shared by the highest and the lowest intelligences, Slim and Lennie. Both individuals represent in their own ways the reality of

38

goodness as an active principle in the world, the goodness arrived at through the travails of experiences and the goodness of innocence.

CROOKS AND THE RANCH HANDS: Significantly, we learn that only two men have ever visited Crooks' room before. The boss, of course, owns the room; it is perhaps not too much to say that he owns Crooks as well. His attitude toward the stable hand, as we have seen, is proprietary. We know, without being told, that the elements that underlie his relationship with Crooks include the vicious sense of racial superiority and power, always present in potentiality, that Curley's wife brought up as her withering threat against the Negro. We also know, without being directly informed, that this sense of superiority can be transcended only with great moral effort and difficulty, that it is a virulence probably shared by every white man on the ranch, to various degrees. That Slim has been the only other guest of Crooks reinforces the reader's belief in Slim's capacity for such a transcendence. Without having been a party to any meeting between Crooks and Slim in the harness room, we can assume, without forcing credulity, that Slim's innate courtesy and detachment would probably operate as they did in the conversations with George.

LENNIE'S VISIT: The key, or one of the keys, to Lennie's functional resemblance to Slim is suggested by the very wording of the initial conversation between Crooks and Lennie. When the Negro hand asks Lennie what he wants in the harness room, Lennie answers, "Nothing...I thought I could jus' come in and set," whereupon Crooks merely "stared" at him. Conditioned by decades of rejection, insults and contempt, the Negro is ready to meet almost any gambit except the unexpected one of free offers of companionship. While it is true that Lennie goes to the harness room out of the experience of loneliness, it is equally true that no learned hatreds or stances of superiority forbid that visit. The processes of socialization include the processes of indoctrination. Since Lennie remains relatively immune to the first, he continues also unblemished by the second. This aspect of Lennie's characteristic nature might very well be a romantic invention on the part of the novelist. However, by presenting Lennie in this way, Steinbeck again forcibly reminds us of his deep-lying suspicions of social artifice.

Thus, we can more readily understand an absolutely basic aspect of Steinbeck's entire career: his unwillingness to treat a complex urban setting. He will write heroic historical romances like *The Cup of Gold*, or novels dealing with men in special, restricted and controlled environments, cells adhering together, one might say. And we come face to face with the biologist's observed world again.

Since, within this biological view of the world, a possibility for good exists, it is interesting to speculate about the conditions in which the good is able to function. A most important element involves giving up the desire to meddle with others' lives. This renunciation is a distinct factor in Slim's make-up. It is equally a factor in Lennie's arrival at Crooks' harness room. But the big man, not through will but through the impersonal processes of fate, does interfere in George's life in a continuous and major way. That George shoulders this burden willingly, we know; that he intermittently complains about it, and bitterly, we also know. Consequently, the narrative fills the reader with more and more foreboding of doom for Lennie. Such a prophecy is implicit in the story of Lennie's misadventure with the girl in Weed; the interest shown in Lennie by Curley's wife; the destruction of Candy's dying dog because the animal is biologically inferior, no good to itself, and a smelly intrusion into the life of the bunkhouse. Nevertheless, insofar as Lennie can be motivated by kindness, to that degree he is not only a man who can initiate human communion, but one who can breed it in others.

CROOKS' CHARACTER: As Slim is a kind of nucleus for the social cell that composes Part III, so Lennie is a sort of nucleus for the world composed of Crooks, Candy, Curley's wife and himself. But there are complicating factors; primary among them is the resurgence of an almost sadistic malevolence on the part of the stable hand. A man who has almost never been treated as an equal by men will experience enormous difficulty in accepting the offer of friendship. Thus, Crooks' initial invitation to Lennie to ''set a while'' leads very quickly to a situation in which the stable hand attempts to assert his newfound sense of power by baiting and frightening the big man. Lennie, who begins as a figure of friendship, suddenly becomes for Crooks the perversely defined symbol of white man's oppression. Crooks is a victim of the sudden departure of his own rational processes. As Lennie's generosity brings forth Crooks' invitation, so Lennie's weakness invites Crooks' buried furies. The pressures are great that condition the insulted and the injured. And those pressures unfortunately tend to bring out, not the noblest elements in a man's nature, but the frightened child and the vengeful self. As an instance of this truth, sociologists have observed departures from the kind of behavior that might rationally have been expected of inmates in German concentration camps during World War II. The unbelievably cruel and inhuman treatment accorded to those inmates might make the reasonable man expect concerted and unified action on the part of the prisoners faced with extinction. But the sad truth all too often was the reverse. A significant number of prisoners, pressured beyond their capacity for communal action or even communication, informed on their fellows and even aped the mannerisms of some of their S.S. guards.

STEINBECK AND CHILDHOOD: Another interesting aspect of Steinbeck's feeling about social artifice relates to the novelist's attitude toward childhood. Soon after Lennie's entry into Crooks' harness room, the Negro stable hand tells him about his childhood. Crooks was born in California. His father had a ten-acre chicken ranch. White boys and girls would come to play at the ranch and "some of them was pretty nice." Crooks tells Lennie that his father did not like such camaraderie, but Crooks asserts that he did not know until much later why: "but I know now," he adds. When he was a boy, his family was the only Negro family for miles around and now he says, he is the only Negro on this entire ranch. With the comparison between the society of his childhood and that of his present situation, Crooks evokes a Steinbeckian belief clearly or covertly present in many of the novelist's works. It is the belief in a kind of purity of motivation in the child's world. Black and white children can play together, perhaps even love each other, but black and white adults must of necessity hate each other. The point goes further than merely an indication of sickness between races; the entire adult world is accused of guilt and complicity. The careful reader of Steinbeck's works can find, besides Lennie, at least two other characters of that level of intelligence and of chronological age, creations that

41

might be another indication of the novelist's continuous concerns. Although Slim proves that it is not a general rule, the reader often feels that as a man becomes good, so he also becomes a child. There are overtones of Christian doctrine implicit in such concepts. "And a little child shall lead them." Indeed, a paper has been written on Steinbeck's use of Christian symbolism. But it is certainly not sufficiently consistent, particularly in this novel, to warrant further attention here.

PART V

Summary

It is Sunday afternoon. In the great barn the horses are resting, nibbling wisps of hay; the flies buzz, cutting through the lazy afternoon. Outside, the men play horseshoes. In the barn, Lennie is stroking the puppy, dead by the thoughtless force exerted by the big man's hands. Lennie is talking, both to himself and to the dog. He is, by turns, both sorrowful and angry at the puppy for having died.

Curley's wife enters the barn. She is wearing her bright dress and the shoes with red feathers. He sees her and panics, shovels hay over the puppy. He rejects her offers of conversation, quoting George's admonitions, but finally shows her the puppy. She consoles him. But Lennie is miserable. George won't let him have any rabbits now because he did a "bad thing." She moves closer, first getting angry at Lennie as she hears him give George's warning about talking to her. Then she switches gears and tells Lennie about an actor from a travelling show, and another man "from pitchers" who would have put her into the movies. The trouble was that her mother probably stole the letters from the latter. So she married Curley. She comes yet closer as she tells Lennie a secret she never had communicated to anyone: "I don't *like* Curley. He ain't a nice fella." Lennie keeps talking about rabbits and she feels insulted: doesn't he ever talk about anything except rabbits? He tells her about the dream house and how he likes to pet soft things. That she can understand. Who doesn't like to pet soft things? Like velvet, for instance... or hair. She invites him to feel her hair. He does. He strokes harder. She cries out. She screams. His hand closes over her mouth and nose. She writhes violently and as his hand lifts a bit, she screams. Lennie grows angry, afraid she'll get him into trouble, just as George had said. He shakes her. She struggles. He shakes her again. He breaks her neck.

He partially covers her up with hay. He remembers about hiding down by the brush near the pool in case of trouble. As he creeps out of the barn, he picks up the dead pup and puts it under his coat. A sheep dog catches the dead scent of Curley's wife and whimpers. Old Candy comes by looking for Lennie, to talk about possible profits from the rabbits. He blunders

43

onto Curley's wife and apologizes; no answer. He tells her she shouldn't sleep there. And then he jumps up and leaves the barn quickly. The horses stamp, chew their bedding and clash their halter chains. Candy comes back with George, who asks the purpose of Candy's bringing him. George sees the body. What should be done? George thinks they have to go get Lennie: "the poor bastard'd starve." Maybe "they" will lock him up and be nice to him. But Candy thinks they should let Lennie get away because Curley's going to want a lynching. George agrees. Candy now asks about the dream ranch; could the two of them go? It's all off. George says he'll work his month for the $50 and then go either to a cathouse or to a poolroom.

George plans now. He won't let anyone hurt Lennie, but says no more about that. He asks Candy to announce the news *after* George has got quietly back to the bunkhouse. George wants no shadow of suspicion to fall on him. Candy does as requested. When George is gone, Candy mutters angrily to the dead body of Curley's wife. It is her fault. Everyone knew she'd mess things up; he could have worked in the garden, with the animals; he could have gone to a ball game if he felt like it. His eyes fill with tears as he leaves the great barn. Suddenly, everyone is running to the barn, after Candy's alert. Slim, Carlson, Whit, Curley, Crooks, then Candy and lastly George, who has pulled his black hat down low over his eyes. Slim is the first to reach the body and touches her cheek and her neck. Curley suddenly cries out: it is Lennie; Curley knows that. He must get a shotgun. Carlson says he'll get his luger. They both run from the barn. Slim tells George there's no choice; they must get Lennie. Carlson comes running back. He can't find his luger and accuses Lennie of theft. Curley carries a shotgun in his good hand. George asks Curley not to shoot "the poor bastard," pleading insanity for Lennie. But they will shoot him. Curley says Lennie has Carlson's luger, and Curley cannot be dissuaded. Candy stays with the corpse.

Commentary

This part contains the dramatic high point of *Of Mice and Men*, the catastrophe toward which the entire novel has been building. The author has prepared the reader for this moment by sketching in individual character traits, attitudes and symbolic situations in the course of the first four parts. Such preparations make it possible for the reader to accept the goings-on with a sense of the inevitable.

We might examine this section in some detail therefore, looking first at the interchanges between Lennie and Curley's wife, and then attempting to understand the reactions to the tragedy of all the other characters. If the behavior of the various members of the ranch strains the reader's credulity at this point, it would be clear that the inconsistency of individual reactions will nullify the dramatic powers of the climax. On the other hand, if the reader can find no major fault with the narrative continuity, he will be able to applaud the achievement of the novelist.

THE SETTING AND THE TIME: The setting is not the bunkhouse, but the barn. Steinbeck had to provide an isolated spot for the meeting between Lennie and Curley's wife. But it had to be a place the relevance of which would not seem forced. Why the barn? The reader will recall that Lennie had made an effort earlier in the course of the novel to bring his gift puppy into the bunkhouse. George forbade such an action, among other reasons because Lennie was not to be trusted with those small living things that he so loved to pet. So Lennie has been relegated to the barn, where he was allowed to make occasional visits to the dog. It is dramatically a very appropriate maneuver to have Lennie commit his ultimate folly in a place that his own character structure made necessary.

Again, why was Lennie alone? He had to be alone, certainly, for the adequate resolution of the plot. But this isolation, too, was completely consistent with what we know of his habits and temperament. Lennie is by necessity a loner. He cannot socialize on equal terms with other men. Where are the other men? They are outside, pitching horseshoes. This is not the first time we hear of the hands pitching horseshoes and we have also been told, in passing, earlier, that small bets ride on the game's results, that the men get all involved with their pastime. We remember, as well, that in the previous part all the men with the exception of Crooks, Lennie and Candy had gone to town for men's recreation. Perhaps the murder could have occurred then, if it had not been for the presence of Crooks and the old man. The entrance of Curley's wife into

45

the harness room, and her clear interest in Lennie, had prepared the reader for danger, as have the repeated warnings by George, interspersed throughout the novel. George's influence upon Lennie is weighty. Thus, the novelist had to provide a context within which Lennie would be sufficiently relaxed to allow him to be touched at his most vulnerable point — the obsessive desire to pet soft things. The stable, where the bitch had her puppies, is such a context. And the presence of Curley's wife assuredly does not surprise the reader either. By the time that the fifth part begins, he knows all about her secretive haunting presence around the ranch, and even has come to expect it. We do not know whether she is looking for anybody in particular. But we do know that she has no doubt as to the cause of her husband's mangled hand; and we know that the "accident" has been a realization of her own secret wish to get even with Curley for his meanness. Indeed, one of the first things she says to Lennie in the barn is that he need have no concern with Curley — after all, he could break her husband's other hand, she says.

LENNIE AND CURLEY'S WIFE: What is the quality of the relationship between the two doomed people? Each is the direct agent of the other's downfall. With one exception, however, each one is so immured in his or her own fantasies that the two do not even communicate with each other. They talk, yes, and they even may share the illusion that they are speaking to each other — but it is only illusion. Each one is talking private thoughts aloud; each one is projecting nostalgia or hope or fear, but no exchange takes place. This absence of any meaningful rapport renders the scene almost unbearably moving. Two isolated creatures, each locked in his own subjectivity, pass by each other in an almost complete human darkness. Lennie's predicament is, of course, clear. But what about Curley's wife? Why is she doomed? She is clearly part of that unconnected mass of social decay that has long attracted Steinbeck's attention. She is adrift from the moorings of the middle-class society for which Steinbeck has little sympathy. But she has not met the challenge posed by such drifting in the manner typical of, say, the *paisano* subculture of which we spoke earlier. So she is nowhere, supported by no family, nourished by no fortifying values, defined by no realistic ambitions. For, the past hopes for a career in "pitchers" on

46

which she largely bases her tawdry attractions and her insecure sense of self, are as illusory as her "conversation" with Lennie.

THE OTHERS: Now, let us examine the reactions of the various other members of this small society to the tragedy. One of the elements that strikes the reader as somewhat harsh, perhaps cruel, conceivably inconsistent, is the degree to which cold objectivity and even self-seeking characterize the reactions of various people. But we know that such responses are often defenses against the pain of feeling. And Lennie's act was not of that sort that carries with it great surprise. In addition, we remember an aspect of Steinbeck's world, in which the impersonal processes of life do not stop or delay in the face of individual tragedy. In fact, it is the representative of that sense of the world who is the first to examine Curley's wife's body. Slim goes over to her "quietly" and feels her wrist. He touches her cheek and his fingers explore her neck. Only then does the silence break and do the rest of the men start talking or shouting. Curley is the first one to cry out for vengeance. He has not even a split second of visible regret, mourning or sorrow. His entire vendetta appears to be one that is merely taking advantage of the death of his wife in order to avenge his destroyed hand. Even at that, his anger and righteous outcries do not seem to come from any deep well within, even if it is only the well of vengeance.

Curley is such a coward that he must excite himself into activity. "He worked himself into a fury," the text reads. And all the hidden hostility that Curley had felt in relation to George can now afford to express itself. He gets pleasure from making sure that George becomes part of the lynching posse. And he does not even use George's name when he addresses him: "You're comin' with us, fella." His shrewd mind is even able to furnish an apparently rational excuse for his urging his colleagues that they "give 'im no chance. Shoot for his guts...." To George's plea that Lennie, not being sane and thus not responsible, should not be killed, Curley counters that Lennie has Carlson's luger, a supposition for which no one has any proof.

As for Carlson, he is very much the same man who hounded Candy about the old man's dying dog. Carlson's immediate response to Curley's call for a killer mob is, "I'll get my luger." No other considerations, no intermediary thought processes come between his view of the girl's body and his running for the weapon.

Candy's world has fallen apart. Whatever hopes he might have had of living in the dream ranch along with George last only a few seconds. His first thoughts are for Lennie. He wants him to get away. He even argues with George about that point, stressing Curley's vindictive cruelty. But the old man's "greatest fear" prompts him directly afterward to ask George pleadingly whether the two of them could still go to the "little place." So it isn't clear whether Candy's concern for Lennie is as unselfish as it seems. In the dim recesses of the old man's mind might have strayed the idea that if Lennie were helped to escape, the three men might still find peace together. Ironically, it is Candy who is chosen by Slim to stay behind with the girl's body. And, although the old man is bereft now of all his lately wakened hopes, he can go beyond his own unhappiness at this instant. He squats down in the hay and looks at the dead girl's face, and he thinks of Lennie, now the doomed quarry of a hunt. "Poor bastard," Candy says softly.

DEATH AND RELEASE: Both George and Slim agree that a caged Lennie is an impossibility. The big man simply could not survive such conditions. At least this is their impression, and it makes possible their part in the hunt. But it is, of course, George who is the great sufferer. A certain ambiguity, however, pervades his suffering. Since Lennie alive exists in the cage of his own limitations, and demands the special attention of the weak, death is a kind of release. It is a release in the same sense that Curley's wife's death enabled her to become "very pretty and simple" in the absence of "the meanness and the plannings and the discontent and the ache for attention."

48

PART VI

Summary

The pool of the Salinas River is still. It is late afternoon. Lennie appears from the brush, silently. He kneels by the pool and drinks, then sits on the bank, embracing his knees. He talks to himself, pleased that he remembered this place and blaming himself for his actions. If George doesn't want him, he thinks, he'll just go away. Then he experiences two extremely vivid fantasies, one involving his Aunt Clara, the second a gigantic rabbit. His aunt criticizes him: how nice George has been to him, and how irresponsibly Lennie has behaved; what a good time George could have had without Lennie on his back, and how poorly Lennie has responded to such care. She disappears, followed immediately by the great imaginary rabbit, who insults Lennie, casts doubt on his ability to care for any animals, to remember feeding schedules, and warns Lennie that George will beat him with a stick. Lennie cries out for George, who appears out of the brush. The big man pleads with George not to leave him. George says he won't. Lennie asks if George will give him hell, but all that happens is the recital of The Story, with Lennie again crying out the punch line in triumph.

George asks Lennie to look across the river, up at the mountains. He will tell Lennie The Story with such clarity that the ranch will become almost visible. As he speaks, George takes out Carlson's luger pistol. He looks at the back of Lennie's head. A man's voice calls from up the river and another voice answers. George raises the gun, but drops it again. He goes on with the story. The footsteps are coming nearer. He raises the gun again; his hand shakes but he pulls the trigger. Lennie falls. George throws the gun down. Slim's voice calls for George. Curley sees Lennie on the sand and looks at the fatal wound. Carlson asks how George did it. George, limp and exhausted, simply answers affirmatively to Carlson's suggestions that George had wrested the gun from Lennie and shot him. Slim takes George up the trail. "You hadda, George. I swear you hadda," he says. Carlson wonders what is "eatin' them two guys."

49

Commentary

The first pages of this part contain a series of interesting and dramatically very effective parallelisms. As musical compositions often return at the end to some of the material typical of the beginning, so this Part VI repeats some of the language and the setting of the first Part — with significant alterations. We will detail these appearances.

PARALLELISMS AND ALTERATIONS: The setting is the same as the one that began the novel, the Salinas River pool. Even the adjectives, which are the second and third words in Part VI — "deep green" — can be found in the same order in the first sentence of Part I. Such specific and pin-pointing details, which might be somewhat irrelevant in a novel by Balzac, say, are quite appropriate here. We have discussed previously the poetic elements inherent in the construction of this novel: and poetry is the concern for the right word in the right place, and for the symbolic word. As in Part I, Steinbeck's feeling for nature is manifest in the description of trees and animals at the pool. They are not merely generalized descriptions, but involve such specific names as sycamore, and willow, lizard, snake, 'coon and heron. It is evening in both parts — the novel opens as darkness comes on, and it plays itself out as well in the coming of darkness. But whereas nature is beneficent in Part I — skittering lizards, sitting rabbits, deep-lying crisp leaves — the animal symbolism of Part VI suggests the continuity of those impersonal biological processes that we have discussed previously. A water snake, gliding the length of the pool, reaches the legs of an unmoving heron, who instantly grabs the reptile and eats it. As snakes eat insects, so herons eat snakes. It is simply the truth about the animal world, to which man also belongs, man in the shape of Curley, or George or Lennie. The wind suddenly rushes, as the heron makes its catch, then all is quiet again. The heron stands again in the shallows, "motionless and waiting." Another little water snake swims up the pool.

Now, Lennie, in his sudden approach, is compared to a bear. But, where in Part I he was seen walking "heavily . . . dragging his feet" as a bear does, in this scene he comes as silently "as a creeping bear does." He is still a bear, but a frightened one. In Part I, Lennie "flung himself down"

50

to drink from the pool, snorting into the water "like a horse," but in this last part, the big man "knelt down" to drink. There are no horselike noises now; he is "barely touching his lips to the water." In the first instance, his animal passion for water was so concentrated that he would not have noticed any noise. As a matter of fact, George had to shake him free of the water. In this scene, however, the sound of a little bird skittering over dry leaves causes Lennie immediately to jerk his head up, all attention focussed on the source of the sound. When he finishes drinking, he sits on the bank. He unconsciously emulates his posture in the first part, when he embraced his knees in imitation of George. In fact, the entire scene is largely composed of restatements of past events and attitudes. In this case, we discover not only the parallelism between the beginning and the end, Parts I and VI, but also a recapitulation of elements from other parts of the novel.

Among them, two are most important, and in the context of this final scene most poignant. They consist of the two stories that constitute the symbolic polarities of George's attitudes toward Lennie. Again, as in the case of the shifting parallelisms described above, the effectiveness of the repetitions is enhanced by subtle variations. George, miserably full of the knowledge of his eventual act, is unwilling to scold Lennie. But Lennie, who is attuned to scoldings no less ritualistically than he is to The Story, actually begs George to tell him off, to recount again how easy life would be without Lennie, how George could take his $50 a month and do what he wanted with it. But George cannot finish this scolding and, at Lennie's request, goes on to the final telling of The Story.

SCENE AND SYMBOLS: Thus, the entire last scene, until the entrance of the men, proceeds by way of indicating symbols. There is no direct foretelling of the killing, and the movement unwinds itself almost like a grave, heartbreaking pageant. In this connection, it is interesting to observe that just before George makes his first effort to kill the big man, he takes off his own hat and suggests that Lennie do the same. "The air feels fine," he tells Lennie. On a practical level, George may have made the suggestion in order to have a clear target. But he could have probably done without this last order. There is another overtone here, vague echoes of the symbolic usage that dictates that men remove their hats in church, that

51

they remove their hats in respect. George, as it were, starts mourning for his friend from this point.

LAST WORDS: The final words of fictional works are usually written with care. They constitute an important part of the reader's last impression and must consequently communicate the author's sense of a deep-lying appropriateness. Steinbeck could easily have ended this novel at one of several points and still have established a dramatic finish. He might have concluded with the conversation between George and Carlson, in which George tiredly assents to Carlson's version of the killing. Or Steinbeck might have ended the book at the point of George's departure with Slim, as Slim assures his companion that there had been no choice, that what is, is, that what had to be done was done. However, the novelist chose to finish the novel with Carlson's comment to Curley, "Now what the hell ya suppose is eatin' them two guys?"

Thus, the book ends on a jarring, harsh and cruel note, typified by lack of understanding and empathy. The statement is a token of extraordinary moral denseness, and perhaps by using it in final position the novelist was attempting to get across to the reader a sense of the implacable and dark disinterest of the world in the tragedy of an individual.

Whatever Steinbeck's intent, this last comment leaves the reader with a powerful sense of the world's iniquity.

52

Character Sketches

Lennie

A huge, mentally retarded, tremendously powerful man, probably in his twenties. Nothing is known of his relatives except for an Aunt Clara, who had apparently taken care of him when he was a little boy. None of Lennie's features is sharply defined, his gait is ambling, his appearance shaggy, his eyes pale and large, his shoulders wide and sloping. He walks heavily, dragging his feet as a bear does its paws. His arms hang loosely. When the movie based on the novel was made, the actor chosen for the role was Lon Chaney, Jr., gifted with a huge body and vast experience in playing various monsters in a number of films. The audience's familiarity with Chaney as a monster did no harm to his interpretation of the role of Lennie. There *is* something almost monstrous about the discrepancy between the immensely powerful, hulking body and the pathetic childishness of the mind.

None of the characters in *Of Mice and Men* is presented in very complex psychological perspective, but Lennie, representing an extreme polarity, is capable of only a few attitudes. The main one, of course, consists of his dependence upon George. The reader tends to assume in the beginning of the novel that George's warnings to Lennie to keep completely silent at the new ranch suggest an almost complete inability on Lennie's part to make any sense. But the situation is not that absolute. What *does* typify Lennie is a characteristic that he holds in common with children: a short attention span. He is able to converse with the stable hand, Crooks, for awhile, but the discussion inevitably leads to a consideration of the one obsessive reference point to which the big man always returns, the hoped-for reality of a little ranch somewhere. He is able to converse, if not to communicate with Curley's wife, but the discussion there inevitably leads to the acting-out of his second obsession: the desire to feel and caress soft things.

Thus, within the context of his dependence upon his companion, Lennie's life is primarily bounded on the one hand by an unrealized dream, on the other by an ungovernable tactile compulsion.

On the practical, day-to-day level of manual labor,

Lennie's strength is second to none. His strength and willingness to work are so immense — like his body — that Slim reacts to them almost as he would to forces of nature. In addition, Lennie's good will and "purity" of intention are never in question. His memory operates poorly in terms of his own experience, but he is able to remember — as George explosively points out to him — even such details as particular words and phrases when they come from George's lips. His bodily movements, no less than the processes of his memory, also sometimes take their cue from his companion's actions. Although he possesses an innate animal grace that allows him to creep quietly, he will sometimes go so far in the surrender of a personal co-ordination as to copy, for instance, the exact way in which George puts his arms around his knees in a sitting position.

George

The reader's general sense of George is an understanding of him as an ordinary man, driven into an extraordinary guardianship by the promptings of moral responsibility and a need for companionship. Whether there are more deep-lying and complex motivations in George cannot be definitely inferred from the information given in the novel. But the occasions that elicit from George an opinion about women suggest some of his attitudes. Whenever he talks about Curley's wife, he sees her not only as a great potential danger to Lennie but, in more general terms, as a symbol of a predatory, unprincipled and dangerous sex. And when George speaks of the uses to which he could put his earnings, in the absence of a responsibility for Lennie, he goes out of his way to point out that a relationship with a bought woman is more convenient and satisfactory than any other. The relationship is governed by the clear purpose of both partners and once that purpose has been achieved, there is no more involvement. In fact, there is something in George that may very well be strongly disinclined to *any* personal involvement. His relationship to Lennie, admittedly, is a close one, but more paternal than anything else, and certainly has no place for intellectual involvement.

Physically, George is characterized by features that are clearly defined. He has restless and observant eyes, strong, small hands, thin arms and a bony nose. As to his dealing with the other ranch hands, George is quite capable of sharing the simple camaraderie typical of life in the bunkhouse. He is cautious and, to some degree, suspicious of new situations, and he has a reasonable right to be. His guardianship is always met with surprise, suspicion or even amused contempt.

Curley

As far as one can be specifically singled out, Curley is the villain of the piece, arrogant, a braggart, a bully and a coward. He is the intensification of the vices of his father, whose appearance makes clear the family pattern. Curley is manipulative and insecure, two traits that work along with each other to the detriment of any possible saving graces in his character. The more insecure Curley gets, the greater his need to handle, order and destroy in a constant search for self-confidence. And, since it is a search based upon external reality and others' attitudes alone, it is doomed to failure. Conversely, the more Curley manipulates people, the greater his insecurity, because he is perceptive enough to observe the loathing in which he is held by everyone in the ranch, with the exception of his father. And, thus, although unredeemed by any appearance of warmth or goodness, he is in his way a tragic figure. As Lennie plays out his tortured life between his dream and compulsion, so Curley is doomed to a constant movement between the ravages of his low self-esteem and his need to control others. The reader may, with a certain reasonableness, assume that Curley's reasons for marrying might have included a certain affection; but even in this relationship Curley's temperament allowed him to act only in such a way as to provoke the girl's confidence to Lennie that her husband was "mean." But the degree to which the reader might conceivably take pity on Curley remains minimal in the apparent absence in the boss' son of any significant conflict between "good" and "bad" impulses.

Curley's wife

The wife is marked by the bad taste inherent in her choice of overly heavy make-up, blatantly decorative ostrich feathers and vulgarity in her stance. Also pertinent, however, is the pitiable loneliness that sends her walking all over the ranch, looking for something unfindable. The ranch hands look upon her with suspicion, and emphasize her greed and dangerous seductiveness. But what they are unable to glimpse is her authentic loneliness. This loneliness, in turn, derives its quality largely from her self-love, which is clearly manifest in her conversation with Lennie during the fatal meeting in the great barn. She is so wrapped up in her impossible fantasy of a career in "pitchers," her adolescent glamorizations of a desirable future, that she can not allow herself to understand the nature of the other person, or the nature of the conversation, in which nothing is communicated.

She has in common with Curley a streak of real viciousness and cruelty. This streak is disclosed on several occasions. When she first starts to talk to Lennie in the barn, she talks with pleasure of the possibility that he might break her husband's other hand. But more incisively, because less justifiably motivated, she lashes out at Crooks, the Negro stable hand, when he objects to her trespassing in his room. Ironically, it is just about the only time that she draws upon a deeply held attitude of (white) society in a powerful and concentrated way. Her threats to him, however, mean-spirited and nasty, are effectively delivered. But otherwise she hardly seems to have a sense of belonging to a significant, solid, real social unit. That she is never named in the course of the narrative is an implicit comment upon her position.

Slim

Slim is the "prince" of the ranch, a skilled workman, the moral arbiter of the bunkhouse, a grave, detached and judicious companion. His stride is graceful and his air benign. His social effectiveness and power form an exact counter to Curley's. Where the boss' son consistently attempts to enforce an acceptance of his power by crude and unsuccessful gambits, Slim is able to gain such an acceptance by not claiming anything. By being himself, clearly a figure of integrity and unclouded perceptions, Slim in his quiet way is accepted as an unvoted legislator in times of problems or questionings.

Candy

Candy is an old ranch hand, the owner of a moth-eaten, blind, old smelly sheep dog whose destruction (by the consent

56

of the majority of the workers on the ranch) constitutes one of the leading symbols of doom and biological necessity in this novel. He acts as a "swamper," that is, a general clean-up man around the ranch. He usually carries a broom. He has been demoted to this position not because of incompetence, but because an accident — which cost him his right hand — has made him incapable of ordinary responsibilities. Nothing is known about his past. He is a lonely man willing to pledge all his savings to the purchase of George and Lennie's dream ranch. He is the one who discovers Curley's wife's body, and he is the one who communicates the discovery to everyone else. He is also the one who, because of his affliction and his age, is delegated to stay by the body at the end of the narrative — thus being saved from the necessity of joining the posse on its mission to destroy Lennie.

The Boss

The boss, Curley's father, the owner of the ranch, appears briefly at the beginning of the novel to meet George and Lennie when they report for work. He is not as mean as his son, but the family resemblance is apparent, except that where Curley is slim, the father is short and stocky. (Both he and his son wear high-heeled boots to indicate to the world that they are not laboring men.) He finds it hard to accept the fact that George does the talking both for himself and Lennie and does not disguise his suspicions that George is trying to put something over on him. He accepts them as workers, but warns George that "I got my eye on you."

Carlson

Carlson is one of the ranch hands, identified physically in the narrative by his "powerful" stomach. Although Slim is the man who gives final approval to the destruction of Candy's dog, it is Carlson who, by his untiring pursuit of the point, brings the issue to a head. There may very well be some underlying vindictiveness in Carlson to prompt him to the unceasing suggestions that the dog be killed. When Carlson is putting forth his reasons for the dog's being put away, he gestures toward various parts of the animal's anatomy with his foot, as if the dog were a thing. And, near the end of the book, Carlson's immediate reaction to the discovery of the girl's

57

body is to run to the bunkhouse in order to get out his luger pistol, almost as if Lennie were an animal, too, which must be destroyed. His stance toward the dog and his hurried run for the weapon make it quite understandable that Carlson, in the book-ending quotation, should not be able to perceive George's agony.

Crooks

Crooks, the old Negro stable hand who lives in the harness room, lives an isolated life on the ranch, even more so than any of the other employees. Before Lennie's arrival at the ranch, the only two men ever to visit him in his room were the boss and Slim. And he, himself, never went over to the bunkhouse. His body is like his life. He has been bent, twisted and rejected by the alien white world; and his body is bent and twisted by an accident to his spine in the distant past. He can be cruel, as to Lennie, but is not so far gone that he will not react to warmth and kindliness with some generosity.

Whit

Whit, a young, laboring man with sloping shoulders and a heavy walk, appears only briefly, and primarily during a scene in which he shows Slim a letter of appreciation to a cowboy pulp magazine, written by an ex-worker at the ranch. The episode serves largely as a brief pause in the tense discussions about the fate of Candy's dog.

Literary Elements

Theme

Human Loneliness

We are told in the first sentence of the novel that the men were at the Salinas River, "a few miles south of Soledad." "Soledad" is the Spanish word for "loneliness." The sense of people trying to cope with their own isolation pervades the entire novel. In the first scene Lennie is rhyming off by heart the story his friend has so often told him. He says:

> Guys like us that work on ranches are the loneliest guys in the world. They got no family. They don't belong no place. . . . With us it ain't like that. We got a future. We got somebody to talk to that gives a damn about us. . . . because I got you to look after me, and you got me to look after you, and that's why.

When the two men arrive at the ranch we meet some of these "guys." The loneliness of the casual laborers working on ranches is a theme that recurs throughout the novel. It is poignantly illustrated in the scene where Whit shows Slim the letter. Whit, a young ranch hand, has seen a letter in a ten-cent western paperback. He recognizes the name as belonging to a man who worked with him on the ranch months before. He is pathetically eager to show Slim the letter. Slim can barely remember the man. We learn from Whit that they worked in the same patch of peas and that "Bill was a hell of a nice fella." For the lonely ranch hand this casual connection was important, something to remember warmly.

Together, Lennie and George have managed something more. George is a shrewd man. He has also learned to care for Lennie. These characteristics enable him to create a situation which keeps their lives from being as empty as those of some of the other characters. He complains about the responsibility of looking after Lennie: "If I was alone I could live so easy. No mess at all an' when the end of the month come I could take my fifty bucks and go into town and get whatever I want." Yet he values the friendship. Along with loyalty and physical protection, Lennie provides George with a boost to his ego and gives

59

him a sense of his own superiority and self-worth. George is aware of his own limitations, for as he says to Slim

I ain't so smart neither, or I wouldn't be bucking barley for my fifty and found. If I was bright, if I was even a little bit smart, I'd have my own little place.

The dream of the little farm is also made possible by Lennie. He believes in it so strongly that it starts to seem possible, but this belief is shown to result from Lennie's being so mentally limited. The other characters — the bitterly wise and cynical Crooks is an example — are so bowed down by harsh reality that they cannot sustain the dream, at least not for very long. Whereas Lennie and George have been able to count on each other and to travel together for some time, the other ranch hands have had no such experience. This is not the usual thing in their world. Slim observes that two people are not often seen travelling together, that "maybe ever'body in the whole damn world is scared of each other." Neither Lennie nor George is complete on his own, but together they make up one whole, strong person with both the brawn and the brain to survive.

Crooks and Candy are a well-drawn pair of minor characters. Their isolation is the result of age in one case and racial prejudice in the other. Candy has his old dog and Crooks has his room and his aloof dignity. Both solutions are fragile, however. Candy's dog is shot and Crooks admits that he would like company in his room, because "a guy goes nuts if he ain't got nobody . . . I tell ya a guy gets too lonely and he gets sick." It is the loneliness that each man feels that causes them to want to join George and Lennie on their planned farm.

Finally, the tragedy that occurs at the end of the story is triggered by the loneliness of Curley's wife. Steinbeck did not even give her a name. This emphasizes her complete isolation from the rest of the group and the way loneliness has dehumanized her. She is not a sympathetic character — she can be cruel and vicious, but this simple, shallow woman is also a victim of an empty life. She dreams of Hollywood stardom and dance halls, but she is isolated on the monotonous ranch among a group of men who regard her with suspicion. She, in turn, regards them as a "bunch of bindle bums." Curley's wife has

60

discovered that her husband "ain't a nice fella," so there is no one to care for her or give her life meaning. Her loneliness and boredom lead her to discover that it was Lennie who broke Curley's hand. She then makes advances to the big, simple man. Lennie tries to avoid her, because he is afraid to provoke George's anger. But Lennie has just lost his puppy and so finally moves over to talk to her. They discover that they both like soft things. The vain, lonely girl invites Lennie to feel how soft her hair is. From there, it is only a step to the tragedy.

Structure

Steinbeck intended to write *Of Mice and Men* in what he called the "play-novelette" form, in other words a novel that could be acted as a play with very little rewriting. It was a successful experiment. In 1937, the year the book was published, the play was produced in New York (where it won the Drama Critics' Circle Award) and in 1940 it was made into a powerful film. If we imagine the six chapters in the novel as the scenes of a three-act play, we can clearly see the structure that this "play-novelette" form imposed.

ACT I

| Scene 1 | (Chapter 1) | The river. Thursday at sunset. |
| Scene 2 | (Chapter 2) | The bunkhouse. Friday morning. |

ACT II

| Scene 1 | (Chapter 3) | The bunkhouse. That evening. |
| Scene 2 | (Chapter 4) | Crooks' room. Saturday night. |

ACT III

| Scene 1 | (Chapter 5) | The barn. Sunday afternoon. |
| Scene 2 | (Chapter 6) | The river. Sunday at sunset. |

As in a play, all that we learn about the characters and events come from what we can see and hear. We are exterior observers of the action, and what cannot be seen — thoughts, recollections, dreams — is kept to a minimum. Much of the novel consists of dialogue. When Steinbeck wants to let us know that Lennie has harmed a woman in the past, he has George tell the story to Slim. Curley's obnoxious character is revealed through comments that the other men and his wife make about him. In the barn scene, we hear the men playing horseshoes outside, but we do not see them. There are two exceptions to this. Aunt Clara and the giant rabbit in Chapter 6 are products of Lennie's imagination. Even these interior views, however, are speaking characters which could be acted on the stage.

The dramatic device of foreshadowing is frequently used. The mice Lennie kills, the story about the woman in Weed, the dead puppy — all lead us to anticipate what happens to Curley's wife. Lennie and George talk about this sense of gathering trouble on their first morning in the bunkhouse. "Le's go, George," says Lennie, "Le's get outta here. It's mean here." The shooting of Candy's old dog for the dog's own good foreshadows George's shooting of Lennie to save him from the worse fate of being shot by Curley or locked up in an institution. This foreshadowing creates suspense. We are led to expect future actions so often that we begin to sense that a fatal doom hangs over the characters. The characters themselves assist in creating this effect. They are simple men and all we learn about them is what is necessary to the plot. So the action moves swiftly to an end that we feel we have been expecting right from the beginning.

Steinbeck creates, by his craftsmanship, a tight unity of time and place. The entire play takes place between Thursday sunset and Sunday sunset. All the action is located in four places — the bunkhouse, Crooks' room, the barn and the river. Suspense is intensified by the elimination of unnecessary words or actions. There is a feeling of completeness when the two main characters return to end where they began — by the river at sunset.

Biblical Allegory

The Cain and Abel Story

Steinbeck often experimented with allegory. This is a story, often a fable, in which people and things have a symbolic meaning intended to convey a message. One critic, Peter Lisca, believes that in *Of Mice and Men* Steinbeck was beginning to work out the Biblical allegory (which he later developed much further in his novel, *East of Eden*) based on the story of Cain and Abel. This story raises the question of the responsibility which men, as brothers in the family of man, must take for each

62

other. When Cain was trying to hide from God the fact that he had killed his brother, he asked, "Am I my brother's keeper?" George is not Lennie's brother — although he tells the boss that he is his cousin — but he is in a very real sense his "keeper" and he does in the end become his murderer.

The theme is carried further by the symbolic use of names beginning with "C". These are the sons of Cain, exiled forever from Eden, and condemned to a life of work and worry, trouble, loneliness and violence. No character has a name beginning with "A" since, according to the Bible, Abel had no descendants. Slim is neither an "A" nor a "C". Slim has God-like qualities. He does not have the problems of the other ranch hands. He appears to be above trouble, and they look to him for leadership. It is his decision to have Candy's dog killed, but he does this out of compassion. In the end he is also responsible for encouraging George to make the decision to shoot Lennie, for similar compassionate reasons. Slim takes the God-like responsibility of making decisions for his fellows.

George and Lennie are also special characters. George kills out of compassion and love for Lennie: "I ain't gonna let 'em hurt Lennie." He also kills out of knowledge. He knows it is the least painful possible end for his friend and he knows also that it will destroy his own dream. Lennie also kills, but he is not a Cain-figure. He is innocent of both evil and knowledge. He does not know what he does, and cannot even take responsibility for his own actions. The situation of the two men raises the complex question of love and responsibility for one's fellow man.

The setting adds symbolism to this Cain and Abel theme. The setting is agricultural; we are not shown any scenes of machinery or urban life to distract us from the allegory. The characters are migrant workers, which reinforces the idea that the sons of Cain were condemned to tramp the earth. The farm that they plan on is symbolic of the Eden that is forever denied to them. As Crooks comments:

> Just like heaven. Everybody wants a little piece of lan'. Nobody never gets to heaven and nobody gets no land.

Meaning

Steinbeck, in portraying his ordinary American characters,

63

often touched upon the question of free will. Can humans influence their own destinies and plan their own lives or are they forever at the mercy of the forces around them? Typically, this most eclectic of writers held several views on this issue throughout his writing life.

His theory that understanding what "is" was a difficult enough problem without worrying about "why?" or "how?" — his non-teleological theory — led some critics to regard him as a writer of the naturalistic school. Recently the definition of naturalism has been subject to heavy criticism. However, one characteristic common to naturalistic writers is a mechanistic view of man: the idea that man cannot influence his fate, that there is no ultimate purpose in the individual life or in the universe. Like the itinerant ranch hands, mankind is travelling from nowhere to nowhere.

The critic, Warren French, has a different view. He thinks that Steinbeck's early novels were naturalistic. In addition to his non-teleological, cold, objective view, Steinbeck had a strong emotional sympathy for human beings, especially for the struggles of ordinary working people. We might say that he wanted to see people triumph, but believed that in reality many of them did not. In the California of the 1930s he saw many examples of people being pushed by forces and circumstances they could not control or change. *In Dubious Battle*, the novel he published just before *Of Mice and Men*, described the futile struggles of migrant fruitpickers from the naturalistic, fatalistic perspective.

However, *Of Mice and Men* is different. It ends with the resignation that is typical of a naturalistic novel, but there are features within the novel that illustrate the beginning of a new type, the drama of consciousness, which Steinbeck then carried forward into *The Grapes of Wrath*. The characters do not meekly accept a fate they don't understand, but try to change their own or others lives. Even if defeated, they go down fighting. The important distinction between the two is the extent to which the characters are conscious and aware of what they are doing and what is happening to them. Steinbeck originally intended to call the novel "Something Happened," which would have been in line with his earlier view. *Of Mice and Men*, taken from the poem by Robert Burns, is a more precise title for a drama of consciousness. It tells us that men can and do make plans. These plans may often "gang a-gley," but not inevitably.

64

It is in the attempt to change one's fate, and in an individual's consciousness of his attempt and his choices, that the human drama lies.

To illustrate this point it is the character of George that is important. The naturalistic character usually lives in a dream world made up of vague wishes and desires, with no particular focus. Seen from one point of view, the farm could represent such a vague desire in George's life. Yet George is not a completely unconscious dreamer. We learn that he actually has found a farm that is for sale. He is impractical, true. He and Lennie do not have even close to the amount of money needed. Yet when Candy offers his money George shows himself capable of quick, practical thought.

In the end the dream is destroyed by forces beyond George's control: natural forces — the heredity that created Lennie the way he was — and social forces that made Curley and his wife the way they were and put them and Lennie in a particular place at the particular time. Lennie was not a self-conscious human being. He had no concept of his own motivations, in fact he could not even remember what he had done a few minutes before. His fate is the result of forces totally beyond his control. We see this clearly in the way that George arranges to shoot him so that he does not even know it is happening. Lennie's life and death illustrates a naturalistic and mechanistic view.

However, at least some of the destruction of the dream lay in George's own actions. For him the farm could not exist without Lennie. He says to the unhappy Candy in the barn, "— I think I knowed from the very first. I think I knowed we'd never do her. He usta like to think about it so much I got to thinking maybe we would." This is a problem in George's own character. He needed Lennie to make him a stronger man. He knew this, for as he said immediately afterwards,

> I'll work my month an' I'll take my fifty bucks an' I'll sit all night in some lousy cat house. Or I'll set in some poolroom till ever'body goes home. An' then I'll come back an' work another month an' I'll have fifty bucks more.

He is conscious of who he is and what he is doing. He

65

knows he is a man who tends to drift, like the majority of the men in the only world around him. But he had tried to construct, with Lennie, something different. The two of them had built a barrier against the loneliness common to the ranch hands, and there was even the possibility of hope for the future. Natural forces helped defeat George, but weaknesses within his own character completed his defeat. George's is not a heroic struggle, but we like him because he tries, even though he knows his own weaknesses. It is this conscious struggle that makes him more than just a simple victim of fate.

In the last chapter he does become heroic. He knows what he has to do, although he hates to do it. He cannot just drift away because he has decided not to leave the killing to Curley. He is aware that he is not only killing his friend, but his own chance at a different future. He stands his ground and does it because he has decided it is the thing he has to do. He is conscious of accepting his fate, and it is this consciousness in this sometimes weak, small man that gives the scene its dramatic power.

We can see in the ending the transition between the naturalistic novel and the drama of consciousness. As Slim leads George away to console him, we are given brief, snapshot views of two contrasting characters. Carlson, the insensitive, unconscious ranch hand mutters, "Now what the hell ya suppose is eatin' them two guys?" Slim, on the other hand, can reach out to George because he has a wisdom gained through consciousness.

66

Critical Review

Steinbeck's Statement of Intentions

In the Introduction we learned important biographical facts about John Steinbeck. We also became acquainted with some of the basic philosophical assumptions underlying not only *Of Mice and Men* but the novelist's work in general. The long commentary sections, which followed the brief summaries of plot, went into some detail about the characterizations, formal structure, allegorical and symbolic aspects of the novel. In this connection we might add that Steinbeck himself, in an article for *Stage* magazine published in 1938 (#15) said that his intention in writing *Of Mice and Men* was to write a play in the "physical technique" of the novel. He explained what advantages would accrue. The play, since it avoided stage directions and such, would be easy to read. Since the novel could describe scenes and people, it would make a good visual picture for the reader as well as for the director and actor. The playwright could set his tone "more powerfully" and wandering and discursiveness would be held to a minimum.

This section will be devoted to a summary of critical reactions to this novel. We have already seen that the play was a huge success. What do the literary critics have to say about the book? The range of critical reaction is very large and falls between the extremes represented by John S. Kennedy and Burton Rascoe.

Burton Rascoe

In 1938, Burton Rascoe, an American journalist and critic, wrote an essay, "John Steinbeck," in which he discussed *Of Mice and Men*. We recall that Steinbeck did not attend the première of his play. Rascoe compliments him on his absence, because it seems that a significant proportion of the audience reacted perversely to many of the lines in the opening act of the play. Although the play was, as we know, an immense success, the audience laughed "outrageously" at some of the conversations between George and Lennie, and at Lennie himself. Nethertheless, by the end of the first act, the insensitivity of the scoffers was overridden by the power and pathos of the action and characterization. It is this capacity

67

of *Of Mice and Men* to make a wonder out of most unpromising materials that Rascoe finds infinitely praiseworthy. In fact, he goes so far as to state that Steinbeck here has done a braver thing than Sophocles (the great Greek dramatist) had ever accomplished. And why? Because the writing problem that Steinbeck set for himself was an almost insuperably difficult one.

The Greek dramatists chose mythological subjects already known to the audience; however extreme some of the incidents or characters, they were not alien. Steinbeck used, as the central protagonist of his novel, a man who could be described by police as a "sexual pervert," a "degenerate." He could be seen by a psychiatrist as suffering from both hormonal and psychological deficiencies. And it is this character whom the novelist chose to humanize, to render so sympathetic that his human qualities attract the reader's sympathy and affection.

For Rascoe, the novel discloses all the "spiritual" warmth and concern in the world. He sees the hopes for tranquillity, contentment and security strung out in the length of the narrative "like a Greek choral chant," raising not only Lennie and George beyond the ordinary and dulling round of daily necessities, but also affecting Crooks and Candy similarly. He finds no sentimentality in the work, and emphasizes his sense of Steinbeck's stern realism. He sees George as hard-boiled, but also as a creature possessing imagination and poetry. Rascoe sees Steinbeck's primary philosophical intention as an attempt to picture nature neither as moral nor immoral, but simply as non-moral.

John S. Kennedy

John S. Kennedy, in an essay, "John Steinbeck, Life Affirmed and Dissolved," published in 1951, takes quite an opposite tack. His opinions tend to agree with those expressed at various times by two very influential critics, Alfred Kazin and Edmund Wilson. For Kennedy, as well as for the other two critics, Steinbeck does a great disservice to man's stature by presenting human life and activity in animal terms. We have seen the parallels drawn between Lennie and the bear, for instance. It is this kind of comparison that Kennedy finds spread throughout Steinbeck's work, and that he finds

68

so overly simplistic and destructive of man's moral capacities that he is revolted. He sees the novelist's interest in biology, as it applies itself to his fiction, not a cohesive philosophical underpinning, but a dilution, which constantly saps the potential success of the novels. He takes a position as a Christian critic and accuses Steinbeck of degrading man by denying him free will, by making him no more than a brute ruled by his passions and incapable of significant personal decision. For Kennedy, Steinbeck, in his concern for the large abstractions of life, succeeds only in becoming "soft-boiled." He specifically refers to the "mawkish" pages of *Of Mice and Men* as examples of cheap and facile sentimentalism. Steinbeck, in this critic's view, has fled from reason, and from attributes of reality that are the fruits of reason: proportion and significance.

Frederick I. Carpenter

Frederick I. Carpenter, in the *Southwest Review* of July, 1941, published an article entitled "John Steinbeck: American Dreamer." His basic contention accents the singleness of purpose underlying all of the novelist's work. Carpenter sees this purpose as the desire to communicate the essence of the American Dream in its successive developments. And that dream involves men's wishes to make of America a strong, lasting nation, a place where hopes can be fulfilled and men can be equal and free. This dream is implicit in the conquests, the Indian raids and the new settlements, and it is often soiled by greed and egoism. It is in such books as *Of Mice and Men*, the critic says, that men derive their nobility and stature from their never-ending dream, despite the tawdriness of their conditions. The ranch hands never stop dreaming of something, a little place of their own, beyond themselves. *Of Mice and Men* thus derives its power from the ability of some of the characters — Candy, Lennie, Crooks — to remember the hopes of the American Dream. They become significant because they express the American Dream "in its simplest form."

Woodburn O. Ross

Woodburn O. Ross, in "John Steinbeck, Earth and Stars," published in 1946, admits that the speech and the greater proportion of the actions in the novel conform to realistic traditions. But he believes that *Of Mice and Men* is broken in two by Steinbeck's self-indulgence, a trait that permits the novelist to allow his feelings to dictate to his judgment. Ross considers that Steinbeck's attempt to portray Lennie as "good" derives from the novelist's irrational conviction that what is "natural" is "good." Since Lennie is a moron, and is thus incapable of sophisticated or even rudimentary thought, he is *ipso facto* utterly incapable of artifice, thus "natural." Ross believes that George's feeling for Lennie is not convincing because it is not that "of most men in real life." The critic suggests that Steinbeck, himself, felt a certain fondness for men like Lennie and cites *The Pastures of Heaven* and *The Long Valley* as containing stories about similar men. But Steinbeck's personal fondness, according to Ross, blinded him to the probable reality of social circumstances. The world Steinbeck would present to the reader is simply not the world in which the majority of people live. Ross emphasizes Steinbeck's beliefs that man cannot be controlled by reason, that virtue seems to be most prevalent in the poor and disinherited.

Edwin Burgum

In 1946, which also marked the appearance of Ross' essay, the magazine, *Science and Society*, published an essay by Edwin Berry Burgum entitled "The Sensibility of John Steinbeck." Burgum, in this critical piece, cites Steinbeck as the writer who presented in the totality of his work the greatest variety of attitudes toward the poor. Burgum sees Steinbeck as operating within a great polarity of attitudes, some of which realistically and generously perceive the authentic dimensions of their condition, some of which descend to the rank trivia and betrayals of honest craftsmanship, which mark the appearance of sentimentality. Burgum's most interesting reference to *Of Mice and Men* includes an examination of Lennie. This critic says that the reader's reaction to the story, and his acceptance of it, depend upon his attitude to George and Lennie, but more specifically to Lennie. And, it is in Lennie that a mystery rests, for the novelist has left the big man's motivations obscure. In Burgum's opinion, Steinbeck attempts to seize upon the

70

reader's sense of the mysterious and his capacity for awe by letting Lennie's mental processes remain in the half-light of confusion and dusk. Although Burgum admits that some readers will find, in the creation of Lennie, Steinbeck's typical approach toward sentimentality, he nevertheless stresses the fact that "no character in Steinbeck is more characteristic of his peculiar talent." The critic sees in Lennie a fit symbol for the hopelessness and confusion of the impoverished in the economic swampland of the thirties and late twenties.

Summary

These paraphrases of critical opinion over the years constitute a sample of the main attitudes, pro and con, that the novel has elicited. More than any other important contemporary American writer perhaps, Steinbeck has his critical reputation constantly in some danger. Richard Chase's book on the American novel, which has become very influential, hardly mentions Steinbeck; two well-received anthologies of critical prose on American writers contain essays on Faulkner, Hemingway, Wolfe, Fitzgerald and other contemporaries, but none on Steinbeck. The awarding of the Nobel Prize to Steinbeck caused a furor of disapproval. But it is likely that a number of his books will stay in the canon of lasting works. And among those that remain, we may probably count the book that at least one critic has called "a little masterpiece" — *Of Mice and Men.*

Review Questions and Answers

Question 1.
What is the structural function of The Story about the dream ranch?

Answer
First of all, it is the most significant bond between Lennie and George. No real equality of intelligence or perception is possible between the two men. And George's guardianship, which he inherited from Lennie's Aunt Clara, his position as surrogate parent, are not by themselves enough to solidify an ongoing relationship. Something more is needed, and is provided by The Story, which is the one shared concern able to involve both men. It is the one factor that tends to initiate a companionable rather than a familial relation. And, thus, it involves aspects of George's character beyond that of mere watchdog, with the result that his final shooting of Lennie gains in poignancy.

Secondly, The Story introduces a "reversal" into the narrative. One of the main elements singled out by Aristotle in his analysis of Greek drama was precisely this "reversal," which added tension and surprise to classical tragedy. The reference is relevant, since a number of critics have pointed out the dramatic virtues of the novel, its applicability for the stage and its sense of the tragic. The point will become clearer if the reader recalls that The Story, in the initial stages of the novel, sounded very much like a necessary fantasy. Suddenly, the discussion between Lennie, George and Candy reveals the fact that the dream ranch may indeed be a real ranch, that somewhere, in a particular place, a particular person was willing to sell a particular ranch for exactly $600. This new knowledge shocks the reader and prepares him for another level of narrative continuity. But, subsequently, the deep and underlying suspicion that the dream ranch could, under no circumstances, find realization intensifies the irony.

In the third place, The Story serves the very useful purpose of bringing together individuals who otherwise would have remained at best superficially friendly acquaintances. The dream ranch is a symbol that brings together the fraternity of the dispossessed — Candy, Lennie and Crooks. By contrasting

72

their hopes with their present conditions, the dream ranch allows the reader to adequately perceive the enormous distance between desire and reality.

And finally, the dream ranch functions so continuously as an important symbol that its appearance in the last scene assumes a significance so great that it changes its quality. The counterpoint between George's last narration of The Story and the death of Lennie by the storyteller's hand suggests a mysterious overtone through which — in spite of the tragic sense of the scene — Lennie's death becomes almost a transfiguration.

Question 2.

Why had Steinbeck originally intended to title this novel *Something that Happened*?

Answer

The answer to this question brings up one of the novelist's most deeply held beliefs. By using this title, Steinbeck meant to imply that concepts of good and bad, being humanly created, were thus insufficient to explain the workings of nature and fate. Nature does not operate according to moral categories. It simply operates; it *is*. Steinbeck termed this attitude "non-teleological," an adjective that means that things do not happen for any particular reason; they simply *are*. And the better part of wisdom is to accept this truth and live in the present without concern for what causes what. According to Steinbeck's thought, especially as it is set forth in *Sea of Cortez*, it is precisely this frenetic search for reasons, for causes, that causes a great deal of trouble in the world. The title, *Something that Happened*, would communicate Steinbeck's sense that Lennie's fate, however tragic, was merely another episode in the larger context of nature and fate.

Question 3.

What does Steinbeck mean by "group animal" and "group memory," and why are these concepts significant in relation to *Of Mice and Men*?

73

Answer

In the course of his investigations of marine invertebrates with the biologist, Edward Ricketts, Steinbeck observed that certain primitive forms of life banded together in a special way. Individuals lost their identity to some degree in becoming part of the larger mass, which could exercise survival techniques more successfully than individual members left to themselves. The novelist reasoned from this biological observation that group memory was also possible, and generally made analogies between the rudimentary animal world and the human world. An interesting aspect of *Of Mice and Men* is the strange anonymity of most of its characters. We learn one or two superficial facts about someone, and get no further information. And even these facts sometimes seem to exist on the level of caricature. For instance, the boss is almost a stock comic parody of The Capitalist: short, stocky, absurdly dressed and querulously suspicious. The people on the the ranch have no past; they have little complexity. And, here, the relevance of the concept of "group animal" becomes clear. Since the individual can be absorbed into the whole, and since the impersonal processes of nature stand outside the fret and worry of individual failure and success, the novelist may be justified in ignoring in-depth portrayals of his characters.

Question 4.

In what way can this novel be placed in a central and continuous tradition of the American novel?

Answer

The critic, Richard Chase, has suggested tradition in the American novel, differing significantly from tradition as usually understood in the English novel, and a second line of American fiction. He has pointed out that the novel in England has ordinarily concerned itself with the activities of individuals within a highly compartmentalized, relatively closed and hierarchical society. In a country where class distinctions are clear and have the sanction of age, the novels that desire to portray that culture adequately must have their settings in a recognizable social context. American society, on the other hand, is marked by tremendous social flux and the pressure of its democratic character. Such a writer as James Fenimore

74

Cooper, whose *Leatherstocking Tales* helped to immortalize the male adventurers of America's early frontier days, is not primarily concerned with the presentation of a carefully stratified society. His heroes do not move in such environments; they move in the woods; they fight Indians; they break trails; and they move largely without women. Although Steinbeck does have a concern for the society of the bunkhouse, it is largely a "biological" concern, not an interest in the study of an ancient and continuing social institution like, say, the British peerage. And although Steinbeck is interested in the poor, he often dooms them to remain in their poverty, superior in virtue, and permanently detached from the vices of the middle class. We can see operating in the life-styles of George and Lennie, the wandering, womanless men of the frontier tradition. They have changed, of course, and radically. The geographical frontier is gone and so is the old derring-do; and so are some of the old simplicities. But the careful reader can still sense in this novel the ghostly and nostalgic presence of the picaresque American tradition. Curley's wife, after all, doesn't even have a name.

Question 5.

Some critics believe that they can find in a novelist's biography certain facts relevant to his artistic attitudes. Can Steinbeck's life give us any clues?

Answer

More than most novelists, Steinbeck has in his fiction stayed "close to home," as it were. He continually exploits the California region where he was born, worked and went to school. He is not an urban person; he did not live in large cities as a boy and tended to distrust them when he got older. An early trip to New York filled him with dissatisfaction. A trip he took around the United States in middle age typically avoided the large cities. This almost congenital mistrust of such places as New York and Chicago has restricted the range of his literary adventures in a period when the most pressing and complex human problems often manifest themselves in urban settings. On the other hand, his affectionate scrutiny of natural processes has enriched a good number of his books. And his empathic identification with the life of childhood has made

75

possible the creation of not only men-children like Lennie, but moving young people like Jody in the lovely story *The Red Pony.*

Question 6.
Compare George and Slim.

Answer
Perhaps the most important distinguishing factor between the two men is the matter of serenity. In other terms, we may see it as self-acceptance and the inward peace derived from such acceptance. All the men on the ranch silently accept Slim as their leader, because, among other things, Slim is the only hand who appears to have a self-confident direction. In actuality, it is not so much his sense of purpose which makes Slim radiate leadership, as it is his comfortable acceptance of the moment. George always thinks about the future. Where will he work next? Can the dream house become a reality? How? In what ways can he protect Lennie from presently non-existent troubles? How will he handle sarcastic taunts about his guardianship of the big man? Although some of these considerations stem directly from George's assumption of responsibility for another person, others derive from George's character structure. He would probably be a worrier in other circumstances as well. Of course, his very involvement with his "ward" marks him off from Slim, who works alone and lives in a kind of compassionate isolation. Another important factor differentiates the two men. George has no special craft abilities; he works reasonably well but does not stand out. Thus, his job is no source of special pride or satisfaction. He must look elsewhere for these qualities, which all men require in at least some small amount. Slim, on the other hand, has a reputation as a craftsman. And the fact that he does not throw his superiority into his colleagues' faces gains him respect and deference.

Question 7.
What is Steinbeck's concept of the middle class?

Answer
Many generalizations have been offered in attempts to answer this question. But the matter can only be discussed

within the context of Steinbeck's own definition of the "middle class." He usually conceives of it in opposition to the multitudes of disinherited, homeless, rootless, drifting, nomadic, impoverished men and women who are the main characters of his most important books. The important protagonists in the novel *In Dubious Battle* are most often workers whose inferior working conditions force them to strike. *The Grapes of Wrath* features as primary characters economically depressed families, owning almost nothing, driven to despair or transcending that despair by the laughter allotted to the utterly miserable. The two main figures in *Of Mice and Men* own nothing, come from nowhere and seem to be going nowhere; one of them is even mentally retarded. Such characters, in the long run, do become Steinbeck's "heroes," a category they enter into when they manage to survive their environment. Thus, if these individuals are in some sense heroes, their "middle class" opposites tend to become — when Steinbeck is being simplistic — villains. The two men in *Of Mice and Men*, the boss and Curley, his son, to whom the reader is clearly the least sympathetic, may be defined largely in opposition to the large roster of likeable or praiseworthy individuals to be found in much of the novelist's fiction. The two men own a ranch, which the younger will likely inherit; they are not drifting here and there; they are not impoverished; they are not rootless; they are not homeless. An interesting speculation may be made at this point. Suppose George, Lennie and Candy *had* managed to set up housekeeping in a ranch of their own — would they have become "middle class"? It is symptomatic that Steinbeck should have kept the threshold of their ambitions at a low level. After all, what they wanted was merely a few rabbits, a little land, a couple of animals and perhaps even the chance of going to a movie occasionally. One almost feels that larger desires would, in Steinbeck's sense of things, have turned the three men into greedy operators rather than leaving them dreamers. Thus, Steinbeck's sense of the world seems to have necessitated the death of the dream, if not the death of the dreamer as well.

Question 8.

How does the socio-economic reality of the late 1920's manifest itself in *Of Mice and Men*?

77

Answer
Many books, rather loosely classified as "proletarian" novels, were written during this general period and into the 1930's as a direct result of the plight of the poor and downtrodden. Steinbeck manages to project this concern in a good number of his books. In addition, however, they sometimes go beyond a simple and sentimental mourning for the underprivileged, and they rarely, if ever, get stuck in the vise of a particular ideology. Steinbeck's feeling for nature in its oneness, his admiration for the objectivity of the biologist's observations — although they can sometimes lead into a syrupy mysticism — can often save him from the rigid and categorical excesses of such economic stances as Marxism, a trap that lured and destroyed some of his fellow writers.

Question 9.
Why did Steinbeck write this novel in the third person?

Answer
Written in a period during which such an important writer as Faulkner, for instance, was desperately trying to invent new forms for the communication of very complex psychological insights into behavior, Steinbeck's *Of Mice and Men* appears at first glance almost a retreat into the formal past. He makes no attempt to delineate in depth the complex and inconsistent motivational patterns of individuals. He writes almost as if Freud never existed. But he is writing not so much a "novel" as an older form, perhaps a fable or an allegory, in which the essentials of personality are presented, and not the complex and meandering highways and byways of individual psychology. It is interesting and rather appropriate that this novel should at times be discussed in relation to Greek tragedy, because the ancient Greek heroes — although complex personalities — existed before the historical period in which the very roots of people's wishes were continuously analyzed so finely that they shattered into a million shards of emotion, intellect and will. Faulkner, for instance, in *The Sound and the Fury*, tried with every imaginative resource at his disposal to represent the inward workings of an idiot's mind. Technically, he attempted to accomplish this purpose by scrambling the idiot's memory pattern. That is, the poor individual can make

no distinctions between what happened yesterday, twenty years before, or in the present moment. The result, for the reader, is a prose so difficult to read that it requires repeated study before he can have even the slightest idea of what is happening. Lennie, too, suffers from an inability to think clearly, to remember. The reader has almost no *inside* knowledge about Lennie's mental operations. Thus, the novel loses in psychological immediacy and modern tonality. But perhaps its fablelike, ancient storyteller's procedure has its own fictive compensations.

OTHER NOVELS

In Dubious Battle

Introduction

With the possible exception of *The Grapes of Wrath*, *In Dubious Battle* is the most successful proletarian novel yet written in the United States. More sharply focussed than the former, and more vivid in its characterizations, its effect is probably more forceful. Although the story springs directly from the clash of social and economic forces during the early part of the depression decade, it remains considerably more than a propaganda piece. An intensely vital narrative, exhibiting both the social awareness and artistic craftsmanship of the author, this book stands among the best of Steinbeck's novels.

Plot Summary

Jim Nolan's father was a workingman driven to his death by the blows of police clubs and pistol butts. As a youngster, Jim witnessed both his father's courage and his despair. He saw his mother lose even her religious faith as poverty and starvation overwhelmed the family.

Older, but still keenly remembering his youth, with the scars of brutality and starvation deeply embedded in his heart, Jim Nolan became a member of the Communist Party. He was assigned to work with Mac, an able, experienced organizer. Together, they became fruit pickers, at a time when the fruit growers had cut wages even lower than the workers had thought possible. A strike was brewing and Mac and Jim determined to hurry it along and to direct its course.

Luck was with them. Shortly after their arrival at the camp of the workers, Mac, by giving the impression that he was a doctor, helped Lisa, the daughter of the camp leader, give birth to her baby. Word of his accomplishment spread throughout the area. After Mac and Jim became friendly with London, leader of the camp, and the other workers, they persuaded the fruit pickers to organize and to strike for higher wages and better living conditions. This was not easy to do. As

80

usual, the orchard owners had made effective use of communism as a social evil. Furthermore, the vigilantes were a constant menace, not to mention deputies, troops and strikebreakers, all hirelings of the fruit growers. In addition, the authorities could always close down the camp by maintaining that it violated the sanitation laws and was a menace to public health. There was also the problem of money and food. The poor migrant workers desperately needed work to supply their daily necessities.

But at last a strike was called. On the night that the strikers were to sneak out to meet the strikebreakers called in by the owners, Mac and Jim were ambushed by vigilantes. They succeeded in escaping, but Jim was shot in the arm. Word of their plan for the next morning had leaked out, and they suspected that an informer was in their midst. Nevertheless, the next day they marched out to meet the strikebreakers at the railroad station, and to implore them not to fight against their fellow workers.

Although the police had assembled in force, they seemed afraid of the strikers. During the encounter, Joy, an old and crippled comrade, was shot and killed. The strikers carried the body back to the camp and, over the body of their comrade, Mac delivered a fiery and eloquent speech, encouraging the strikers to carry on and to fight to the finish. This action proved to be the best of all possible spurs to bring the workers together, and the strikers were aroused to carry on the struggle even more fiercely.

Luck was with them in other ways. They had persuaded the father of Al Townsend, who owned a lunch cart and gave handouts to Party members, to allow them to camp on his farm, after they promised him that his crop would be picked and that his property would be protected. Doc Burton, a philosopher and sceptic, took charge of the sanitation, thus protecting the camp against the health inspectors. Dick, a handsome comrade, used his charms on women in order to get money and food for the strikers.

Meanwhile, the owners tried everything to break up the strike. They attempted to intimidate the workers, to divide them, to bribe London, but all their efforts failed. Then another problem arose. The owners had an article published in which it was stated that the county was feeding the strikers.

81

The report was not true, but those who sympathized with the strikers believed it and stopped helping them altogether. Dick was getting far fewer results from his endeavors, and the situation became desperate.

Mac was often on the point of losing his head, of letting his anger get the best of him, so that the strategy of the strike was sometimes imperiled. By contrast, Jim grew more able, more hardened. He ignored the women of the camp who sought to lure him into their tents, and did not allow his feeling for Lisa to become anything more than a casual, friendly relationship. Thus, he provided a sort of balance for his emotional comrades.

Conditions grew worse. The strikers had practically no money and no food. Dick finally managed to get a cow and some beans, but the food sufficed for only a few days. Meanwhile, Doc Burton had vanished. Without his help, the sick and the wounded could not be attended to, and the sanitation of the camp grew progressively worse. One night someone managed to outwit the guards and set a barn on fire. The barn and a adjacent kennel, housing some favorite pointers, were totally destroyed. The next day, the owner called in the sheriff to evict the strikers.

The strike seemed lost. The spirits of the men were at a very low ebb, and they gave signs of yielding. On the following night, a boy came and told Jim and Mac that Doc Burton was lying wounded in a field. They rushed out, only to realize when they were fired upon, that they had fallen into a trap. Mac called out a word of warning and fell to the ground. When he got up, after the firing had stopped, he called out to Jim. He got no answer. Jim was dead. By that time the shots had aroused the others and they came forward. Over the body of his comrade and friend, Mac made a strong and rousing speech, urging the workers to stick together, to fight on and to win the strike.

Principal Characters

Mac, a communist labor organizer who organizes a fruit pickers' strike. After many hardships, in the face of starvation and imminent eviction, the strike seems doomed. Then Mac rallies the strikers with a stirring speech over the body of one of his fellow comrades.

82

Jim Nolan, the friend and co-organizer who is finally killed. The son of a workingman whose death was caused by policemen's blows, he has come to communism by way of starvation and early ill-treatment.

London, the leader of the fruit pickers.

Doc Burton, a philosopher and sceptic. He does much to maintain the sanitation of the camp and the strikers' health during the strike. Things worsen after his disappearance. It is in response to a report that he is lying wounded in a field that Jim and Mac rush out into the trap in which Jim is killed.

Al Townsend, the owner of a lunch cart. He gives handouts to the strikers, for whom he feels sympathy. His father permits the strikers to camp on his farm.

Lisa London, the daughter of the camp leader. Mac's influence around the camp greatly increases after he, giving the impression he is a doctor, helps Lisa give birth to her baby.

Joy, an old and crippled comrade who is killed in an early conflict. Mac's speech on this occasion does much to unify the workers.

Dick, a handsome comrade who uses his charms on women in order to get food for the strikers.

The Red Pony

Introduction

In 1937, *The Red Pony* was republished with "The Leader of the People" as its fourth part. It has since become one of Steinbeck's most popular works and is generally acknowledged as a classic story of childhood. In 1948, Steinbeck wrote a film script of *The Red Pony* for Republic Pictures. The resulting film was considered an artistic success. Paperback versions of *The Red Pony* have gone into many printings, with sales totalling millions of copies.

The Red Pony is probably the most autobiographical of Steinbeck's work, along with portions of the much longer *East of Eden*. But the autobiographical element is one of nostalgia rather than transcription of actual events and persons. It is an imaginatively realized evocation of a childhood, at once idyllic and biologically real. Its relation to Steinbeck's own childhood appears in its being set in an unspecified past. There are no automobiles, and Grandfather's reminiscences appear to place it somewhere between 1910 and 1920.

Plot Summary

The action takes place chiefly on Carl Tiflin's ranch in the Salinas Valley. It is a place of ceaseless life-and-death struggle, of an appalling carnage, which Steinbeck introduces at all points but so subtly and unobtrusively that it can easily escape the reader's attention except as atmosphere. Such passages as "Jody heard the hoot-owls hunting mice down by the barn ..." occur by the dozen and form a running commentary on the meaning of the action, in addition to serving as atmospheric detail.

Steinbeck very cleverly employs contrasting symbols in the story. At the brushline, there is a stream of spring water spilling into a tub and making the grass around it perpetually green. This is the place Jody seeks out when he is troubled or confused, above the tame and ordered ranch and contrasting with the black cypress tree where pigs are killed at slaughtering time. To Jody, the water tub and the cypress are "opposites and enemies." These symbols are associated with Jody's struggle to understand.

In Part I, "The Gift," Jody receives the pony as a gift

from his father, but through the hired hand Billy Buck's "mistake" about the rain, it dies. The title is ironic, for Steinbeck means to imply that a pony bought but *unearned* is a bad gift. In Part III, "The Promise," Bill says that Jody should raise a colt: "It's the *only* good way." Throughout Part I, Jody is treated ambiguously: he loves and cares for the pony but twice falls asleep during his watch over it. He sees himself raised up over the other boys by his possession of the horse, as a hero who has not earned his heroic stature. The action shifts from ranch house and kitchen to school, to stable, to the brushline in a series of pastoral episodes that lend variety of scene, while the drama of the pony's death and Jody's natural response in the killing of the buzzard draws to a close. The rising importance of Billy Buck in the boy's true education is seen throughout.

In Part II, "The Great Mountains," Jody's progress toward understanding continues. His own vague stirrings toward the heroic are symbolized by the Great Mountains to the west, as contrasted with the safe, populated Gabilan Mountains to the east. Gitano, an old *paisano*, comes to the ranch to ask for space to die, in exchange for a few chores. He is refused by Jody's father, Carl Tiflin, who sees him as a used-up and useless object, like the ancient horse, Easter. Jody and Billy Buck both react with kindness to Gitano, who "steals" old Easter and rides away to die in the Great Mountains. The Great Mountains symbolize the heroic past and, like Gitano, with his natural dignity and his secret, sacred sword, arouse the nameless longing for wonderful deeds in the boy. Jody moves closer in spirit to Billy in this short chapter, learning compassion for the dignified old man, and feeling a surge of the "westering" drive that Steinbeck sees as the group feeling of the great days of the pioneers. The mountains are used as a psychological focus — Jody is thrilled at the thought of exploring them, but his father (ironically) takes pride in their being unexplored. For the boy, as for Billy and Gitano, the unknown is a challenge; for the father, a threat. The action takes place about half a year after the death of the red pony.

Part III, "The Promise," begins about nine months after Part II. Jody is coming home from school and envisions himself at the head of a phantom army, which dissolves in mist a few moments later. The passage can be dismissed as a boy's

85

fantasy, charming but inconsequential, but, for Steinbeck, it is something more than that. Again, the theme of heroism is sounded in this touching and beautiful image. Again, there is the suggestion, so common in Steinbeck, of racial memory, the unconscious dream of a heroic past, a trailing of Wordsworthian clouds of glory.

Horses, lambs, old sheep and calves graze in a wonderfully evocative picture of spring in the valley. Jody imagines menacing bears and tigers on the hillside, but Steinbeck makes a wry, indirect comment on the unlikelihood of a heroic life for Jody by having him collect bugs and toads in his lunch pail rather than killing tigers. He is still called the "little" boy.

Jody is given a second and better chance at a colt, this time by taking the mare, Nellie, to be bred. Carl Tiflin makes the offer at Billy's suggestion. Again, Jody dreams of nameless wonders he will perform with the new colt but, this time, he must wait nearly a year for its birth. Billy promises to see that it is a good birth — "The Promise" of the title.

In the birth scene, with disaster as overhanging and real as in Part I, Billy is forced to kill Nellie in order to deliver the colt and keep his promise to Jody. The scene of the colt's birth and Nellie's death is stupendous, one of the great realistic passages in American fiction and the emotional climax of *The Red Pony*. Once again it marks a step in Jody's passage toward understanding. Instead of rejoicing in the colt as a possession, he is struck by sympathy and gratitude toward Billy.

Part IV, "The Leader of the People," is a decline in the action of *The Red Pony* but a further development of Jody's humanity. His grandfather visits the ranch, a heroic figure from an earlier generation. Like Gitano, he is enormously dignified, and Jody is drawn to him. He is described as having such a "granite dignity...that every motion seemed an impossible thing," the likeness to a statue again emphasizing his heroic nature. His great days are long since past, the "westering" days when the group chose him almost automatically as the leader, and he is cruelly ridiculed by Jody's father. In the painful episode in which he overhears Carl deriding the glorious past, Grandfather tries to make clear what it was like to have been the "leader of the people." Here, Steinbeck once more presents his group theory of society acting like one organism, a theory re-echoed in *The Pearl* when the town is likened to a "colonial animal" whose parts are less important than the collective whole. *The Red Pony* closes on a quiet note, when Jody selflessly comforts his grandfather with a lemonade.

As in the other parts of the story, Steinbeck uses natural detail for both setting and symbol. The proposed hunt for mice in last year's straw is treated realistically, but is used as ironic contrast to the Indian fights and terrors of Grandfather's passage west.

The plot of *The Red Pony* is loosely knit, the four parts connected psychologically but not by a single action. Moreover, each of the four parts proceeds in a leisurely, almost rambling way until a crisis or emotional intensification occurs. Parts I and III are slow-paced accounts, first, of the training of the red pony and, second, of the year-long gestation of Nellie. In each part there is a sudden almost desperate quickening at the crisis — the death of the pony and the birth of the colt — that is highly effective, like the crashing of a storm after a long calm.

Principal Characters

Billy Buck is the hired hand on Carl Tiflin's California ranch. He is short, stout, competent with his hands, good with animals and perceptive. He is not the central figure of the novel, but he is perhaps closest to being its hero. Billy Buck also serves as something of an intermediary between Jody and his father. Billy is, at all times, a strong figure, and, as a character, would probably rank as one of Steinbeck's more successful creations. He is visually vivid with his walrus moustache, his worn belt and his ancient hat with pieces of straw sticking in the band for picking his teeth. Billy's quiet heroism is defined by his familiarity with elemental forces. His "mistake," which leads to the pony's death, is very possibly meant as an unconscious protest against the easy commerciality of the pony as gift.

Jody, the boy with the red pony, is an attractive but somewhat ambiguous character. Like Huckleberry Finn, he is torn between the life of nature and the restrictions and prohibitions of respectable middle-class life as represented by his parents. Like Billy Buck, Jody has an intense sympathy with the animal world but, unlike Billy, he is given to spasmodic fits of cruelty and destructiveness.

Jody is, on the whole, very sympathetically drawn. His response to the old *paisano*, Gitano, who has come home to die, and to his grandfather is gentle and understanding. He is torn between the freedom represented by Gitano and the heroism of Grandfather on the one hand, and the restrictiveness and middle-class responsibility of his parents on the other. His awareness of the conflicting forces pulling at him is made evident in a number of places, one of the most direct being the sentence: "Jody rejoiced for he knew that only a mean-souled horse does not resent training." His slow, faltering growth toward understanding is completed by the touching small gift of lemonade for his grandfather but not himself.

Carl Tiflin, Jody's father, is the least sympathetic character in *The Red Pony*. He is represented more as being obtuse and rigid than as positively bad, however. He is described again and again by Steinbeck as "stern" to indicate a certain rigidity. His impulses of generosity of spirit are always, as Steinbeck sees him, somewhat spoiled by the conditions he attaches to his gifts. His failure to understand his son is the mark of his middle-class entanglement in the problems of "civilization," that is, of getting and spending. When Jody, in a dark rage, destroys the buzzard, Carl Tiflin fails to perceive the symbolic justice of the act. When Gitano asks for only a little space in which to live out the end of his days, Carl Tiflin refuses, even though the cost would have been minimal for him. When Grandfather comes for a visit, Carl Tiflin is sarcastically offensive in Grandfather's presence and insulting while he is away. There is a quality of emotional awkwardness about Carl as Steinbeck portrays him, a fear of seeming soft when he makes generous and kindly gestures.

Mrs. Tiflin is both the competent, sympathetic mother who appears repeatedly in Steinbeck's work and a mild authority figure. It is she who most often and directly reminds Jody of his duties but, in moments of crisis for the boy, she becomes quietly understanding and helpful.

Gitano is a symbolic character representing that large class of outcasts, vagabonds and *paisanos* to whom Steinbeck is so powerfully drawn. His name, which means "gypsy," gives a

88

clue to his unsettled existence. In his confrontation with Carl Tiflin, whom he asks to allow him to stay on the land of his birth for the short period before his death, Gitano is notably dignified. There is a suggestion of a parallel between Gitano and Steinbeck's much-loved Arthurian heroes. He is discovered to have a sword that is sacred to him. He departs for the dark mountains to die on an ancient horse, like an old warrior in a medieval epic.

Grandfather is the old hero, the shadow of the generation that conquered the West. His virtues are those of the more natural generation, and he is the embodiment of Steinbeck's religious and biological imagination. In recalling the glorious days when he was the leader of the westward-moving pioneers, Grandfather speaks in characteristically biological terms. Steinbeck's view of the group, as an organism that moves like one animal and that selects its leaders automatically, appears in the image of Grandfather. Steinbeck's belief in mystical group-drives is seen in Grandfather's lament over the end of the "westering." Like the other members of his weakened generation, Grandfather stands on the seashore and curses because there is nowhere further west to go. Grandfather represents a level of heroism that Jody can never attain in a tamed world. There is an interesting and moving prefiguring of this in the striking passage in which Jody marches at the head of the vast unseen army that dissolves in mist.

The Grapes of Wrath

Introduction

In *The Grapes of Wrath*, Steinbeck has achieved an interesting contrapuntal effect by breaking the narrative at intervals with short, impressionistic passages, recorded as though by a motion-picture camera moving quickly from one scene to another and from one focus to another. The novel is a powerful indictment of our capitalistic economy and a sharp criticism of the Southwestern farmer for his negligence in the care of his land. The outstanding feature of *The Grapes of Wrath* is its photographically detailed, if occasionally sentimentalized, description of the American farmers of the Dust Bowl in the 1930's.

Plot Summary

Tom Joad was released from the Oklahoma state penitentiary where he had served a sentence for killing a man in self-defense. He travelled homeward through a region made barren by drought and dust storms. On the way he met Jim Casy, an ex-preacher. The pair went together to the home of Tom's family. They found the Joad place deserted. While Tom and Casy were wondering what had happened, Muley Graves, a die-hard tenant farmer, came by and disclosed that all of the families in the neighborhood had gone to California or were going. Tom's folks, Muley said, had gone to a relative's place preparatory to going west. Muley was the only sharecropper to stay behind.

All over the southern Midwest states, farmers, no longer able to make a living because of land banks, weather and machine farming, had sold or were forced out of the farms they had tenanted. Junk dealers and used-car salesmen exploited them. Thousands of families took to the roads leading to the promised land, California.

Tom and Casy found the Joads at Uncle John's place, all busy with preparations to leave for California. Assembled for the trip were Pa and Ma Joad; Noah, their mentally backward son; Al, the adolescent younger brother of Tom and Noah; Rose of Sharon, Tom's sister, and her husband, Connie; the Joad children, Ruthie and Winfield; and Granma and Grampa

90

Joad. Al had bought an ancient truck to take them west. The family asked Jim Casy to go with them. The night before they started, they killed the pigs they had left and salted down the meat so that they would have food on the way.

Spurred by handbills that stated that agricultural workers were badly needed in California, the Joads, along with thousands of others, made their torturous way in a worn-out vehicle across the plains toward the mountains. Grampa died of a stroke during their first overnight stop. Later, there was a long delay when the truck broke down. Small business people along the way treated the migrants as enemies. And, to add to the general misery, returning migrants told the Joads that there was no work to be had in California, that conditions were even worse than they were in Oklahoma. But the dream of a bountiful West Coast urged the Joads onward.

Close to the California line, where the group stopped to bathe in a river, Noah, feeling he was a hindrance to the others, wandered away. It was there that the Joads first heard themselves addressed as *Okies*, another word for tramps.

Granma died during the night trip across the desert. After burying her, the group went into a Hooverville, as the migrants' camps were called. There they learned that work was all but impossible to find. A contractor came to the camp to sign up men to pick fruit in another county. When the Okies asked to see his licence, the contractor turned the leaders over to a police deputy who had accompanied him to camp. Tom was involved in the fight that followed. He escaped, and Casy gave himself up in Tom's place. Connie, husband of the pregnant Rose of Sharon, suddenly disappeared from the group. The family was breaking up in the face of its hardships. Ma Joad did everything in her power to keep the group together.

Fearing recrimination after the fight, the Joads left Hooverville and went to a government camp maintained for transient agricultural workers. The camp had sanitary facilities, a local government made up of the transients themselves and simple organized entertainment. During the Joads' stay at the camp, the Okies successfully defeated an attempt of the local citizens to give the camp a bad name and thus to have it closed to the migrants. For the first time since they had arrived in

California, the Joads found themselves treated as human beings.

Circumstances eventually forced them to leave the camp, however, for there was no work in the district. They drove to a large farm where work was being offered. There they found agitators attempting to keep the migrants from taking the work because of unfair wages offered. But the Joads, thinking only of food, were escorted by motorcycle police in to the farm. The entire family picked peaches for five cents a box and earned in a day just enough money to buy food for one meal. Tom, remembering the pickets outside the camp, went out at night to investigate. He found Casy, who was the leader of the agitators. While Tom and Casy were talking, deputies, who had been searching for Casy, closed in on them. The pair fled but were caught. Casy was killed. Tom received a cut on his head, but not before he had felled a deputy with an ax handle. The family concealed Tom in their shack. The rate for a box of peaches dropped, meanwhile, to two-and-a-half cents. Tom's danger and the futility of picking peaches drove the Joads on their way. They hid the injured Tom under the mattresses in the back of the truck and told the suspicious guard at the entrance to the farm that the extra man they had had with them when they came was a hitchhiker who had stayed on to pick.

The family found a migrant crowd encamped in abandoned boxcars along a stream. They joined the camp and soon found temporary jobs picking cotton. Tom, meanwhile, hid in a culvert near the camp. Ruthie innocently disclosed Tom's presence to another little girl. Ma, realizing that Tom was no longer safe, sent him away. Tom promised to carry on Casy's work in trying to improve the lot of the downtrodden everywhere.

The autumn rains began. Soon the stream that ran beside the camp overflowed, and water entered the boxcars. Under these all but impossible conditions, Rose of Sharon gave birth to a dead baby. When the rising water made their position no longer bearable, the family moved from the camp on foot. The rains had made their old car useless. They came to a barn, which they shared with a boy and his starving father. Rose of Sharon, bereft of her baby, nourished the famished

92

man with the milk from her breasts. So the poor kept each other alive in the depression years.

Principal Characters

Tom Joad, Jr., an ex-convict. Returning to his home in Oklahoma after serving time in the penitentiary for killing a man in self-defense, he finds the house deserted, the family having been pushed off the land because of drought and in order to make way for more productive mechanization. With Casy, the preacher, he finds his family and makes the trek to California in search of work. During labor difficulties, Tom kills another man when his friend Casy, who is trying to help the migrant workers in their labor problems, is brutally killed by deputies representing the law and the owners. He leaves his family because, as a "wanted" man, he is a danger to them, but he leaves with a new understanding, which he has learned from Casy: it is no longer the individual that counts but the group. Tom promises to carry on Casy's work of helping the downtrodden.

Tom Joad, Sr., called **Pa,** an Oklahoma farmer who finds it difficult to adjust to new conditions while moving his family to California.

Ma Joad, a large, heavy woman, full of determination and hope, who fights to hold her family together. On the journey to California she gradually becomes the leader of the family.

Rose of Sharon Rivers, called **Rosasharn,** the married, teen-age daughter of the Joads. Her husband leaves her, and she bears a stillborn baby because of the hardships she endures. As the story ends, she gives her own milk to save the life of a starving man.

Noah, the slow-witted second son of the Joads. He finally wanders off down a river when the pressures of the journey and his hunger become too much.

Al, the third son of the Joads. In his teens, he is interested in girls and automobiles. He idolizes his brother, Tom.

Ruthie, the pre-teen-age daughter of the Joads.

Winfield, the youngest of the Joads.

Uncle John, the brother of Tom Joad, Sr. He is a lost soul who periodically is flooded with guilt because he let his young wife die by ignoring her illness.

Grampa Joad, who does not want to leave Oklahoma and

93

dies on the way to California. He is buried with little ceremony by the roadside.

Granma Joad, also old and childish. She dies while crossing the desert and receives a pauper burial.

Jim Casy, the country preacher who has given up the ministry because he no longer believes. He makes the trek to California with the Joads. He assumes the blame and goes to jail for the "crime" of a migrant worker who has a family to support. He is killed as a "red" while trying to help the migrant workers organize and strike for a living wage.

Connie Rivers, Rosasharn's young husband, who deserts her after arriving in California.

Floyd Knowles, a young migrant worker with a family, called a "red" because he asks a contractor to guarantee a job and the wages to be paid. He escapes from a deputy sheriff who is attempting to intimidate the workers. Tom Joad trips the deputy and Jim Casy kicks him in the back of the head.

Muley Graves, a farmer who refuses to leave the land, although his family has gone. He remains, alienated and lonely, forced to hide, hunted and haunted.

Jim Rawley, the kind, patient manager of a government camp for the migrant workers.

Willy Feeley, a former small farmer like the Joads. He takes a job driving a tractor over the land the Joads farmed.

Ivy Wilson, a migrant who has car trouble on the way to California with his sick wife, Sairy. The Joads help them and the two families stay together until Sairy becomes too ill to travel.

Sairy Wilson, Ivy's wife. When the Wilsons are forced to stay behind because of her illness, she asks Casy to pray for her.

Timothy Wallace, a migrant who helps Tom Joad find work in California.

Wilkie Wallace, his son.

Aggie Wainwright, the daughter of a family living in a boxcar with the Joads while they work in a cotton field. Al Joad plans to marry her.

Jessie Bullitt, Ella Summers, and **Annie Littlefield,** the ladies' committee for Sanitary Unit Number Four of the government camp for migrant workers.

94

The Pearl

Introduction

The Pearl was first implanted in Steinbeck's mind as an anecdote. He and Ed Ricketts made their sea voyage on the "Western Flyer" in March and April of 1940, travelling to the Gulf of California off Mexico. Although the trip was primarily for collecting marine specimens, Steinbeck and Ricketts enjoyed their trips ashore at small Mexican towns. At one of these, La Paz, he was told a story "of recent years," about an Indian boy who finds a great pearl that brings him nothing but disaster, much as the pearl in Steinbeck's story does. The boy eventually throws the pearl away and is restored to a happy life.

Steinbeck marvelled at the anecdote and found it hard to believe as a report of an actual event. He says of the Indian boy that he is " ... too heroic, too wise.... In every way he goes contrary to human direction. The story is probably true, but we don't believe it; it is far too reasonable to be true."

The story is described as "a parable," which means that it has its origins not in the tradition of the novel but in religious and folk literature. (Several years later Steinbeck told of his aim to give it the "set-aside, raised-up feeling" of folk stories.)

The parable form, of course, puts the author in a different relationship to, and at a greater distance from, his characters. Their psychology becomes necessarily simplified: Kino's mental states are almost entirely strategies for dealing with enemies. He and Juana are seen from farther away, as it were, even farther than Jody in *The Red Pony*, who develops perception through individual struggle and sympathy, while Kino acquires the authority of his manhood through ritual struggle.

Plot Summary

The plot of *The Pearl* is one of taut unity. After a very brief awakening scene in which the quality of the family life is quietly established, events move rapidly. The whole is bound together by the evil presence of one unifying object, the pearl itself.

The reader is apprised at once that the form of *The Pearl* will be that of parable. The implications of this for character

95

development are obvious: the figures will have universal rather than particular significance. The plot implications are not so obvious, although, as in biblical parables, the reader can expect to arrive at a moral lesson and to be entertained by a simple story.

Steinbeck changed some details of the tale he heard in La Paz, making Kino a married man with a family rather than a boy, and keeping the pearl with him on the flight from the pursuers rather than hiding it. Otherwise it is largely the same tale.

Kino, a pearl fisher, finds an enormous pearl that he expects will bring him comparative wealth. It will give him enough money for perpetual masses, a marriage ceremony, a rifle and an education for his child. Instead, it brings him nothing but evil. All the parasitical elements of the town work first to cheat him, then to rob him. He flees the town with his wife and child to seek a better price for the pearl, but he is pursued by killers who track him as far as a waterfall. There, he kills the pursuers, but the child is killed by a rifle shot. He and his wife return to their town and exorcise the evil by throwing the pearl back into the sea.

The setting is the tropical seacoast of Baja California. Kino awakens amid the sound and sight of roosters, pigs and little birds to begin a day's search for pearls. A moment later, a goat approaches, a moth flies into his house, ants move about on the ground and his dog comes along to greet him.

Steinbeck's interest in drama has often been noted. Not only has he written several plays and a number of film scripts, but he also thinks dramatically in some of his prose fiction. *The Pearl* is such an example. The stage is set with a quiet introduction to the family's three members. It is a quiet morning, full of peace and "wholeness." The serenity is symbolized by the Song of the Family, an internal melody in Kino's mind, like a racial memory signifying peace and contentment.

Almost at once the tranquility is shattered by the presence of a scorpion, whose appearance brings out the Song of Evil. The scorpion stings the child and the action is begun. Spurned by the corrupt doctor of the town because they have nothing of value to give, Kino and Juana must fall back on folk remedies, which ironically prove adequate. As if fated to do so,

Kino, in his crisis, finds "the pearl of the whole world." The news travels magically through the town as if it were a single organism (Steinbeck's familiar biological figure), and the evil of the pearl is let loose.

At the news of the pearl, "The poison sacs of the town began to manufacture venom, and the town swelled and puffed with the pressure of it." In short, it has the effect on the town that the scorpion's poison has had on the baby, Coyotito.

For Kino, the Song of the Pearl is, at first, compatible with the Song of the Family. He and Juana are filled with hope. The fears of the town are, however, truer than Kino's dreams of glory.

A series of misfortunes follows on Kino's possession of the pearl. He is offered an absurdly low price for it, he is visited by the parasitical doctor and priest, he is attacked, his boat destroyed and his house burned down. The greatest disaster, however, is his loss of family authority — Juana being more intuitive sees the evil of the pearl and tries to destroy it, thus defying Kino's position as head of the family. He reasserts his authority by beating her, and she follows him with the child in his attempt to find a better price away from his home town.

They are pursued in a superbly taut chase scene. The story unfolds rapidly to its tragic, but purifying, conclusion when Kino returns with Juana to the town to resume the old way of life, thus parablelike, completing the circle of the action.

The incidents of action follow one another at a breathless pace. The chapter of flight and return is one of almost intolerably sustained suspense up to the point where Kino kills the pursuers and the baby dies. This is the climactic scene toward which every incident has been drawn in an ever quickening tempo.

Principal Characters

Kino is differentiated from his fellow fishermen merely by his finding the pearl. Like them, he is seen as a victim of the commercial class and, as an *Indio*, of the Spanish elements in the town. The Spanish (the doctor, the priest and the pearl buyers) are presented as the evil element in the lives of Kino and his brethren. Like his fellow *Indios*, too, Kino's identity is largely established by his reactions to his oppressors. His dislike and suspicion of the doctor, his patient irony over the priest's sermon about staying in one's place, his distrust of the pearl buyers, all these are class rather than individual reactions. He has the courage, the seriousness and the endurance of his class. Kino, then, is a universal figure, set apart from his fellows by the accident of his discovery of the pearl.

Juana is defined as a character by her position as wife and mother. She is another of the many competent mother figures appearing throughout Steinbeck's work. She, too, is not a developed character but is seen as having the qualities and virtues of her class and biological function. Her perception of the evil of the pearl is not highly individualistic and not at all intellectual, but is a function of her intuitive family consciousness.

The elemental and universal aspects of the story are seen in the savage incident where Kino knocks Juana to the ground. The evil of the pearl is made slowly known to him through his misadventures, and he eventually destroys it himself. The fact that Juana had attempted to destroy it secretly shows that, for her, it is a threat superseding her natural function as the obedient one in the family. The restoration of Kino's authority in the family is seen at the end when she refuses his offer to let her destroy the pearl and insists that his position gives him the right to do so instead. Juana is a simple figure illustrating Steinbeck's ideas of the family as an ecological unit — her identity derives from her biological function in the ecological unit.

The doctor is the chief black figure in this black and white parable. He represents the oppressive quality of the commercial class at its worst. He is unhealthy, self-indulgent, cruel, greedy, hypocritical and very incompetent. His evil qualities stem from his unnatural (that is, unbiological) function. He is seen by Steinbeck as a parasitical element in society and is related to four hundred years of oppression of the *Indios*, going back to the conquistadors of Cortez. Oddly, the doctor is probably the figure closest to a developed character in *The Pearl*. His small indulgences, his daydreams about the life of ease and sensuality in Paris add interest to him as a character, although they are somewhat unparablelike in the vividness of their detail.

The pearl buyers are indistinguishable from each other in morals or function, like the arms of a single organism. All pearl buyers, as Steinbeck sees them, are defined by their professional objective, which is to pay the smallest price for the most valuable pearl. The first pearl buyer met in the story is made colorful by his habit of running a coin over his knuckles, and his bargaining scene with Kino is masterfully done as Steinbeck concentrates on his hands and their nervous movements. Like the other pearl buyers, he is a black figure, that is, unnatural because he is commercial.

Juan Tomas and **Apolonia,** Kino's elder brother and his wife, are used as part of the action in providing shelter for Kino, Juana and Coyotito after their house is destroyed. Juan Tomas, as the elder, has family authority over Kino. Apolonia, a minor character, illustrates Steinbeck's conception of the individual as part of the group, with her former lament when Kino and his family are presumed dead.

The pursuers are black figures, not individualized at all except that one rides a horse while the other two walk. They are drawn as shadow figures of a nightmare menace. They are a personification of the force with which society puts down challenges to the status quo.

East of Eden

Introduction

East of Eden is an ambitious but not altogether successful attempt to present three themes simultaneously: a panoramic history of the Salinas Valley (and thus of America itself) around the turn of the century; a melodramatic chronicle of two families in the valley; a symbolic recreation of the Cain and Abel story. Its expressed concern, however, is philosophic — the nature of the conflict between good and evil. In this conflict, love and the acceptance or rejection it brings to the individual plays an important role, yet one has always the opportunity to choose the good. In this freedom lies man's glory. The book's defects stem from the author's somewhat foggy and sentimental presentation of its philosophy, and his tendency to manipulate or oversimplify characters and events for symbolic purposes.

Plot Summary

The soil of the Salinas Valley in California is rich, though the foothills around it are poor and its life shrivels during the long dry spells. The Irish-born Hamiltons, arriving after American settlers had displaced the Mexicans, settled on the barren hillside. There, Sam Hamilton, full of talk, glory and improvident inventions, and Liza, his dourly religious wife, brought up their nine children.

In Connecticut, Adam Trask and his half-brother, Charles, grew up, mutually affectionate in spite of the differences in their natures. Adam was gentle and good. Charles was roughly handsome with a streak of wild violence. After Adam's mother had committed suicide, his father had married a docile girl who had borne Charles. Adam loved his stepmother but hated his father, a rigid disciplinarian whose fanatic militarism had begun with a fictitious account of his own war career and whose dream was to have a son in the army. To fulfil his dream, he chose Adam, who could gain the greater strength that comes from the conquest of weakness as Charles could not. But Charles, whose passionate love for his father went continually unnoticed, could not understand this final rejection. In violent despair, he beat Adam almost to death.

Adam served in the cavalry for five years. Then, although he hated regimentation and violence, he re-enlisted, for he could neither accept help from his father, who had become an important figure in Washington, nor return to the farm Charles now ran alone. Afterward, he wandered through the West and the South, served time for vagrancy and finally came home to find his father dead and himself and Charles rich. In the years that followed, he and Charles lived together, although their bickering and inbred solitude drove Adam to periodic wanderings. Feeling that their life was one of pointless industry, he talked of moving west but did not.

Meanwhile, Cathy Ames was growing up in Massachusetts. She was a monster, born unable to comprehend goodness but with a sublimely innocent face and a consummate knowledge of how to manipulate or deceive people to serve her own ends. After a thwarted attempt to leave home, she burned her house, killing her parents and leaving evidence to indicate that she had been murdered. She then became the mistress of a man who ran a string of brothels and used his insatiable love for her to torment him. When he realized her true nature, he took her to a deserted spot and beat her savagely. Near death, she crawled to the nearest house — the Trasks' — where Adam and Charles cared for her. Adam found her innocent and beautiful. Charles, who had a knowledge of evil through himself, recognized the evil in her and wanted her to leave. Cathy, needing temporary protection, enticed Adam into marrying her but, on their wedding night, she gave him a sleeping draught and went to Charles.

Feeling that Charles disapproved of Cathy, Adam decided to carry out his dream of going west. He was so transfigured by his happiness that he did not take Cathy's protests seriously. As his ideal of love and purity, she could not disagree. Adam bought a ranch in the richest part of the Salinas Valley and worked hard to ready it for his wife and the child she expected. Cathy hated her pregnancy, but she knew that she had to wait calmly to get back to the life she wanted. After giving birth to twin boys, she waited a week. She then shot Adam, wounding him, and walked out.

Changing her name to Kate, Cathy went to work in a Salinas brothel. Her beauty and seeming goodness endeared her to the proprietress, Faye, and Kate gradually assumed control of the establishment. After Faye made a will leaving Kate her money and property, Kate slyly engineered Faye's death. Making her establishment one that aroused and purveyed to sadistic tastes, she became legendary and rich.

Adam was like a dead man for a year after his wife left him, unable to work his land or even to name his sons. Finally, Sam Hamilton woke him by deliberately angering him, and Sam, Adam and Lee, the Chinese servant and a wise and good man, named the boys Caleb and Aron. As the men talked of the story of Cain and Abel, Lee concluded that rejection terrifies a child most and leads to guilt and revenge. Later, after much study, Lee discovered the true meaning of the Hebrew word *timshel* — thou mayest — and understood that the story meant in part that man can always choose to conquer evil.

Sam, grown old, knew that he would soon die. Before he left his ranch, he told Adam of Kate and her cruel, destructive business. Adam, disbelieving in her very existence, visited her and suddenly knew her as she really was. Though she tried to taunt him, telling him that Charles was the true father of his sons, and to seduce him, he left her a free and curiously exultant man. Yet he could not tell his sons that their mother was not dead.

Caleb and Aron were growing up very differently. Aron was golden-haired and automatically inspired love, yet he remained single-minded and unyielding. Caleb was dark and clever, a feared and respected leader left much alone. When Adam moved to town, where the schools were better, Aron fell in love with Abra Bacon. Abra told Aron that his mother was still alive, but he could not believe her because to do so would have destroyed his faith in his father and thus in everything.

About this time, Adam had the idea of shipping lettuce packed in ice to New York, but the venture failed. Aron was ashamed of his father for failing publicly. Caleb vowed to return the lost money to his father.

As they faced the problems of growing into men, Aron became smugly reglious, disturbing to Abra because she felt unable to live up to his idealistic image of her. Caleb alternated between wild impulses and guilt. Learning that Kate was his mother, he began following her until she, noticing him, in-

102

vited him to her house. As he talked to her, he knew with relief that he was not like her. She felt his knowledge and hated him. Kate herself, obsessed by the fear that one of the old girls had discovered Faye's murder, plotted ways to destroy this menace. Although Caleb could accept Kate's existence, he knew that Aron could not. To get the boy away from Salinas, Caleb talked him into finishing high school in three years and beginning college. Adam, knowing nothing of Caleb's true feelings, was extravagantly proud of Aron.

World War I began. Caleb went into the bean business with Will Hamilton and made a fortune because of food shortages. With growing excitement, he planned an elaborate presentation to his father of the money once lost in the lettuce enterprise. First, he tried to persuade Aron, who seemed indifferent to his father's love, not to leave college. Caleb presented his money to Adam, only to have it rejected in anger because Adam's idealistic nature could not accept money made as profit from the war. He wanted Caleb's achievements to be like his brother's. In a black mood of revenge, Caleb took Aron to meet his mother. After her sons' visit, Kate, who was not disturbed by those she could hurt as she was by someone like Caleb, made a will leaving everything to Aron. Then, overburdened by age, illness and suspicion, she commited suicide.

Unable to face his new knowledge of his parents' past, Aron joined the army and went to France. Adam did not recover from the shock of his leaving. Abra turned to Caleb, admitting that she loved him rather than Aron, whose romantic stubbornness kept him from facing reality. When the news of Aron's death arrived, Adam had another stroke. As he lay dying, Caleb, unable to bear his guilt any longer, told his father of his responsibility for Aron's enlisting and thus his death. Lee begged Adam to forgive his son. Adam weakly raised his hand in benediction and, whispering the Hebrew word *timshel*, died.

Principal Characters

Adam Trask, a settler in the Salinas Valley. He marries Cathy Ames in Connecticut and moves west, where he and their twin sons, Caleb and Aron, are deserted by her.

Cathy Ames, Adam Trask's seemingly innocent but evil

wife. Deserting Adam and their twin sons, Caleb and Aron, she becomes the proprietress of a notorious brothel.

Aron Trask, smugly religious, idealistic twin son of Adam Trask and Cathy Ames. Unable to face the knowledge of his parents' past, he joins the army and is killed in France.

Caleb Trask, impulsive twin son of Adam Trask and Cathy. Rejected in an effort to help his father, he takes revenge by revealing to his brother, Aron, the secret of their mother's identity. He later accepts responsibility for the disillusioned Aron's death.

Abra Bacon, Aron Trask's fiancée. Disturbed because she feels unable to live up to Aron's idealistic image of her, she finally turns to the more realistic Caleb Trask.

Charles Trask, Adam Trask's half brother.

Samuel Hamilton, an early settler in the Salinas Valley.

Liza Hamilton, Samuel Hamilton's wife.

Lee, Adam Trask's wise and good Chinese servant.

Faye, proprietress of a Salinas brothel. Her death is engineered by Cathy Ames as she seeks to gain full control of Faye's establishment.

Will Hamilton, business partner of Caleb Trask.

Bibliography

Aaron, Daniel. "Radical Humanism of John Steinbeck: *The Grapes of Wrath* Thirty Years Later." *Saturday Review*, LI (September 23, 1968).

Alexander, Stanley. "The Conflict of Form in *Tortilla Flat*." *American Literature*, XL (March 1968).

Beach, Joseph Warren. "John Steinbeck: Journeyman Artist," "John Steinbeck: Art and Propaganda," *American Fiction, 1920-1940*. New York: The Macmillan Company, 1942.

Beebe, Maurice, and Jackson R. Bryer. "Criticism of John Steinbeck: A Selected Checklist." *Modern Fiction Studies*, XI (Spring 1965).

Chase, Richard. *The American Novel and its Tradition*. New York: Doubleday Anchor Books, 1957.

Donohue, Agnes McNeill. *A Casebook on "The Grapes of Wrath."* New York: Thomas Y. Crowell Company, 1968.

Dusenbury, Winifred L. *The Theme of Loneliness in Modern American Drama*. Gainesville: University of Florida Press, 1960.

Fairley, Barker. "John Steinbeck and the Coming Literature" in *The Sewanee Review*, April-June 1942.

Fontenrose, Joseph. *John Steinbeck: An Introduction and Interpretation*. New York: Holt, Rinehart & Winston, Inc., 1963. In the "American Authors and Critics Series."

French, Warren. *John Steinbeck*. New York: Twayne, 1961. In the "United States Authors Series."

_____. *A Companion to "The Grapes of Wrath."* New York: The Viking Press, 1963.

Frohock, W.M. *The Novel of Violence in America*. Dallas: Southern Methodist University Press, 1957.

Geismar, Maxwell. *Writers in Crisis: The American Novel 1925-1940*. Boston: Houghton Mifflin, 1961.

Hayashi, Tetsumaro. *John Steinbeck: A Concise Bibliography (1930-1965)*. Metuchen, N.J.: Scarecrow Press, 1967.

Hayashi, Tetsumaro, and Richard Astro. *Steinbeck: The Man and His Work*. Corvallis: Oregon State University Press, 1971.

Hyman, Stanley Edgar. "Some Notes on John Steinbeck." *Antioch Review*, II (Summer 1942).

Jones, Lawrence William. " 'A Little Play in Your Head': Parable Form in John Steinbeck's Postwar Fiction." *Genne*, LLI (March 1970).

Kiernan, Thomas. *The Intricate Music, A Biography of John Steinbeck*. Boston and Toronto: Little, Brown & Co., 1979.

Levant, Howard. *"Tortilla Flat*: The Shape of John Steinbeck's Career." *PMLA,* LXXXV (October 1970).

Levidova, I. "The Postwar Books of John Steinbeck." *Soviet Review*, IV (Summer 1963).

Lisca, Peter. *The Wide World of John Steinbeck*. New Brunswick, N.J.: Rutgers University Press, 1958.

Marks, Lester Jay. *Thematic Design in the Novels of John Steinbeck*. New York: Humanities Press, 1969. Originally published as No. IX in "Studies in American Literature," The Hague: Mouton, 1969.

Moore, Harry T. *The Novels of John Steinbeck: A First Critical Study*. Chicago: Normandie House, 1939. Second edition, "With a Contemporary Epilogue," Port Washington, N.Y.: Kennikat Press, 1968.

Richards, Edmund C. "The Challenge of John Steinbeck." *North American Review*, CCXLIII (Summer, 1937).

"John Steinbeck Special Number." *Modern Fiction Studies,* XI (Spring 1965).

Tedlock, E.W., Jr., and C.V. Wicker, eds. *Steinbeck and His Critics: A Record of Twenty-Five Years*. Albuquerque: University of New Mexico Press, 1957.

Watt, F.W. *John Steinbeck*. New York: Grove Press, Inc., 1962. In the "Writers and Critics Series."